Second Edition

High Heels &
Bound Feet

D0144781

Second Edition

High Heels &
Bound Feet

And Other Essays on
Everyday Anthropology

ROBERTA EDWARDS LENKEIT

Modesto Junior College

WAVELAND

PRESS, INC.

Long Grove, Illinois

For information about this book, contact:
Waveland Press, Inc.
4180 IL Route 83, Suite 101
Long Grove, IL 60047-9580
(847) 634-0081
info@waveland.com
www.waveland.com

10-digit ISBN 1-4786-3768-4
13-digit ISBN 978-1-4786-3768-4

Printed in the United States of America

7   6   5   4   3   2   1

To Don

for his endless support, 51 years and counting . . .

and

to Katherine and Aaron, my grandchildren,

for inspiring me (and for those canasta games)

Contents

Preface   ix

1 ~ Culture Is Us   1

2 ~ The 13-Letter Word   9

3 ~ Does Anyone Here Speak English?   17

4 ~ A Long and Boring Day   25

5 ~ The Hospital as Foreign Culture   35

6 ~ The Purple House   45

7 ~ Grass and Class   53

8 ~ High Heels and Bound Feet   61

9 ~ White Teeth   67

10 ~ Fireballs   75

11 ~ Return of the Kitchen Elf   83

12 ~ We Are the Eagles   91

13 ~ "I Do!"   99

14 ~ Zip Your Lip   105

15 ~ Unforeseen Consequences   113

16 ~ Dogs and Cats   121

17 ~ Move!   131

18 ~ Food for Thought   139

19 ~ Who Has the Power?   145

20 ~ Potlatch?   153

21 ~ Human Variation   161

22 ~ Yellow-Billed Magpie   169

23 ~ Ape Bars—Not Monkey Bars   175

24 ~ Sidewalk Fossils   179

25 ~ Bricks   183

References   189

Index   193

Preface

I believe that education should color one's life and make it more interesting; it should broaden one's perspective. This edition continues to examine everyday events from the viewpoint of anthropology—its approach, concepts, and data. I've written for introductory students of anthropology and general readers. My objectives are to show how to make one's world more engaging and provocative by viewing it through anthropology's lens each day—at work, at school, at home, at play; to show myriad possible applications of anthropological concepts to everyday experiences.

Topics and concepts are presented in 25 essays (7 new, 18 carryover) that are loosely grouped to coordinate with topics covered in undergraduate courses in both cultural and general anthropology, with an emphasis on cultural anthropology. Each essay begins with a brief, descriptive introduction and concludes with a question or statement that "challenges" the reader to think deeply about a particular concept discussed in the essay. End-of-essay features—"Thinking It Through," "Anthropological Terms," and "Thinking Practically"—provide a review of key concepts and terms in the essays and stimulate readers to apply anthropological thinking to their everyday lives. These essays, in combination with the challenges and end-of-essay features, are reported by adopters of the first edition to have effectively promoted lively discussions and engagement with concepts in both traditional and online courses. Individual readers have also shared that essays promoted both discussions and debate. As a professor who taught undergraduates for nearly 40 years, I cheered.

The assistance and support of many contributed to this edition. Foremost thanks to my husband and fellow anthropological educator Don A. Lenkeit who again acted as sounding board and in-house editor. Special thanks to fellow anthropologists and colleagues Liz Soluri and Debi Bolter who gave time to read and offer valuable input and suggestions. To Dr. Steven E. Faith O.D. my appreciation for taking the time to review my treatment of visual acuity. To Carolyn Kerr, my thanks for once again providing thoughtful insights and support. Thanks, too, to Katherine Meezan for reading and offering her spot-on critique of several essays. My appreciation extends to Aaron Meezan for his thoughts on dogs and cats and the book cover. As always for her support, thanks to my daughter and colleague K. Allison Lenkeit Meezan. Thanks to Judy Shannon and Kisha for walks sparked with thoughtful discourse. My appreciation also goes to Qi Yue for her insights on culture. Thanks, as well, to Susan Mayall for her reviews and suggestions. And appreciation to the many others who contributed through the years: the members of the California Community College Anthropology Teachers group for the years of stimulating meetings and sharing teaching strategies; colleagues at the College of Marin; Mount Royal College in Calgary, Alberta, Canada; Modesto Junior College; and my former students for their curiosity and inspiration. Thanks to the entire production team at Waveland Press. Special appreciation to copy editor Jeni Ogilvie, it was a pleasure to work with you again. To Waveland Press senior editor Tom Curtin, your enthusiastic support, creativity (those wonderful covers!), and publishing acumen are unequaled, thank you. And for the seventh time my thanks to my gentle writing companion Mr. Darwin (1999–2017), who combined paperweight duty with his usual printer watching for this edition.

1 ~ Culture Is Us

Culture influences us every day. This concept is a central theme in this book and in all of anthropology. Therefore a short primer on culture is presented as a backdrop for the following essays.

Corporate culture, geek culture, police culture, office culture, teen culture, American culture, Egyptian culture, Japanese culture, diplomatic culture, and political culture were all mentioned in one two-hour period tonight as I watched television. As I listened to the talking heads of newscasters and actors delivering scripted dialogue, I was struck by how much the term *culture* is used and how it is assumed that everyone is on the same page regarding the meaning of culture—that we all get it. When I query students on the first day of class as to what is meant by these usages, the overwhelming responses describe culture as "behaviors." I believe that everyone *gets aspects* of the concept, yet the complete anthropological meaning of the term evades most people. Therefore, I offer a short primer on culture and how anthropologists view and use this essential concept.

Culture is us. It defines our species; it is what makes us human. It influences us every day. It has had a profound effect on the evolution of our species. This concept unites all of the study areas within anthropology. We are trained to think holistically—we consider the integrated whole, not just its parts. Hence, we include in our perspective everything about human culture and human biology over an extended time span covering at least five million years. This is reflected in the traditional four fields approach to undergraduate training in anthropology. An undergraduate anthropology student studies the data from *cultural anthropology, linguistics, archaeology*, and *biological anthropology*. The influence and role of culture is a theme in each of these subfields; it is a theme that runs through the essays in this book.

Anthropology as a discipline is, in many ways, like a general contractor who has broad knowledge and coordinates specialists in many areas to achieve a finished building project—architects, electricians, plumbers, cement specialists, framers, drywall installers, tile layers, painters, and others. To draw another analogy, anthropology is like a family practitioner in medicine; she or he must have knowledge in all aspects of medicine to treat patients and make referrals to specialists. Most importantly, the family practitioner focuses on the whole patient, all of the organ systems and biochemistry involved in his or her well-being, including the significant role of psychological factors: The family practitioner orchestrates the care of patients. Both the general contractor and the family practitioner take broad, *holistic* approaches to do their work well. The same applies to anthropology. We emphasize holism as we study humanity, while other disciplines such as economics, history, sociology, biology, and political science focus on specific aspects of humanity. Culture is the concept that links the various specific anthropological studies to create our holistic discipline—the study of humankind both culturally and biologically.

Culture is the central theme in cultural anthropology (including *ethnology* and *ethnography*). Cultural anthropologists focus on human cultures today. Ethnographers are people who *describe* culture by gathering data through doing *participant observation* within a culture; that is, they go into a cultural setting for an extended period of time and observe and describe what they see, hear, smell, and touch. They may also participate to some extent in the culture as they come to know people. Ethnologists pull together data gathered from various ethnographers and *compare and analyze* them.

Linguistic anthropologists study the nature of human language—its structure, history, and social aspects. Archaeologists have as their major aim the establishment of chronologies (cultural sequences) of the past, the reconstruction of past lifeways (past cultures), and the analysis of how cultures change through time. Biological anthropologists study human biological development, diversity, and evolution (necessitating that we also study nonhuman primates for clues to our anatomical and behavioral development).

Culture is unquestionably the primary adaptive mechanism of our species today; data in the archaeological record support the assertion that human culture has been of critical importance to our survival for more than a million years. Hence, culture is an important element in biological anthropology research. It impacted our survival and thus our DNA. Our biological history shows that our ancestors gradually evolved bipedalism, hands with both a precision and power grip, and a bigger brain. Over long stretches of time it was not how fast we ran or the size of our teeth that determined survival. Rather, it was our ability to flexibly adapt to our environment and to transmit everything we learned within our social groups to future generations. Successful individuals survived better and reproduced more than others; over generations this led to an increase in the role of culture for our biological survival.

Since much of what humans made and used was not preserved in the archaeological record, it is likely that what we have as "hard" evidence of culture represents only a small portion of *artifacts* used and made by our ancestors—artifacts that helped us survive. Combine this artifact data with the necessary communication and social organization required to coordinate behaviors and to share and transmit knowledge of acquiring food and shelter and avoiding danger—and the powerful role of culture emerges.

What exactly is culture? "Culture is the sum total of the knowledge, ideas, behaviors, and material creations that are learned, shared, and transmitted primarily through the symbolic system of language. These components create a pattern that changes over time and serve as guides and standards of behavior for members of the society. The term *culture* is used in the abstract as well as to refer to a specific culture" (Lenkeit 2012: 26). The concept of culture is, I believe, anthropology's most important idea.

3

The concept of culture, as defined by anthropologists, has undergone some subtle changes since the latter part of the nineteenth century when it was first introduced. This is not to say that we have changed what we mean by the concept. Rather, the definitional changes reflect our change in focus; the changes in focus are tied to changes in, and popularity among, anthropologists of various theoretical models to explain human cultures.

As the discipline of anthropology was forming in the latter part of the nineteenth century, a popular definition appeared that is still often quoted. E. B. Tylor wrote: "Culture . . . is that complex whole which includes knowledge, belief, art, law, morals, customs, and any other capabilities and habits acquired by man as a member of society" (Tylor 1958[1871]). Variations on this definition appeared over the next several decades.

These definitions listed the various components of culture—culture consists of x, y, and z. In fact, to this day if you listen to a group of anthropologists talking about what they mean by culture, one issue that they would discuss are the various components of culture. Generally, these parts fall into several groupings: (1) *behaviors* such as eating customs, gestures, forms of play, cooperation, food gathering (2) *material objects* such as tools, pottery, clothing, buildings (3) *ideas,* such as knowledge and values and beliefs. In other words, the earliest definitions focused on stating that culture consists of what people *do* and what people *make* and what people *think.*

What people do—human behavior can be observed—from gestures, generalized reciprocity, and gambling to mate selection, manners, and market exchange. Ethnographers gather descriptive data on humans' behaviors in the field (i.e., in a cultural setting) and use the data to write an ethnography. Ethnologists then compare and analyze behavioral data from various ethnographies to write an ethnology. What people make—from artifacts (objects manufactured, altered, or used by humans) to *features* (nonportable evidence of technology such as buildings and other architectural elements, fire hearths, trash pits, artifact clusters) are essentially products of human cultural processes and are at the center of what archaeologists do. What people know, think, believe, and value comprise

4

culture, and while not directly observable, these aspects of culture provide the framework on which other aspects of culture are built. Behaviors typically reflect these aspects of one's culture. For example, if honesty is a cultural value and a people share the belief that it is important, we should be able to observe actual behaviors that reflect this value, for example returning a wallet found on a shop floor in the mall.

In 1952 anthropologists A. L. Kroeber and C. Kluckhohn wrote a book about definitions of culture—it contained an extensive list of definitions and ran over 400 pages. Yet, if one reads this book end to end, as I have, the reader is left with the certainty that all anthropologists are talking about the same thing, but they use different words to describe the concept. The same holds for definitions written in subsequent decades. A cultural anthropologist prefers to include phrases like "shared knowledge and belief," an archaeologist wants to include a term like "artifacts," while a biological anthropologist wants to include words like "ecological adaptation" as they define culture. But *all* share the basic features of the concept, although they express it differently.

In the 1940s and 1950s a shift began in definitions of culture. Leslie White, who wrote expansively on the idea of culture, moved the discussion in a different direction by *focusing* on *how people acquire culture*—the processes of how it is learned. He wrote that culture is "that class of things and events dependent upon symboling, products of symboling, considered in an extrasomatic context" (White and Dillingham 1973: 29). A symbol is something—verbal or nonverbal—that represents something else. Language, both spoken and written, is a symbolic system, the most obvious one that we use. For example the word "table "is a symbol in the English language that represents an object with a flat top and several legs holding it up off of the floor; the symbol for table in Spanish is *mesa*. It is primarily through language that one learns one's culture. Other symbols can include body gestures, objects, and colors. We also learn our culture through observing and imitating others and by trial and error. White emphasized that culture is not part of our genetic inheritance when he used the phrase "considered in an extrasomatic context." *Soma* (a Greek word) means "body." And "extra," as used here, means outside of—so extrasomatic means *outside of the body.* White's definition is important because it expanded how we thought about culture.

The consideration of the *process* by which one acquires and transmits culture reflects major scientific breakthroughs of the time. Prior to the 1940s anyone studying the past, including archaeologists, paleoanthropologists, and geologists could date past events only by a means known as "relative dating." A relative date is limited in that it tells you that one thing is older or more recent than another, but not exactly how old each thing is. If, for example, an archaeological object was found underneath another object, it was considered to be older than the one on top. Thus, scientists who studied the past worked on establishing the correct sequences. They could tell which strata (layer of the earth) or which artifact was older and which was more recent than another in a particular sequence, but they could not give ages in years. This meant that unless there was some way to correlate layers of the earth's crust, or layers of cultural occupation over wide geographical space, they could not say which of two sites was older. This was a particularly thorny problem when one wanted to assess the prehistory of large geographical areas such as Asia, Africa, Europe, or North America. With the development of the radiocarbon dating method (Carbon 14) and other radiometric methods that followed, the age of sites could be compared. This led to increased interest in the cultural process and was more specifically reflected in definitions of culture. (Note: E. B. Tylor's early definition only suggested this in his use of the term "acquired.")

In the 1960s and 1970s definitions emerged that focused on culture supplying humans with *programs* or *blueprints* for their behavior (not forgetting that what people do, make, and think are learned, shared, and transmitted symbolically). Clifford Geertz, one of the proponents of humans' use of programs or blueprints, used a computer analogy in 1973 when he talked of culture supplying "programs" for guiding people's behaviors. One of my favorite statements reflecting this perspective is that of Ward Goodenough who wrote that "culture, then, consists of stan-

6

dards for deciding what is, standards for what can be, standards for deciding how one feels about it, standards for deciding what to do about it, and standards for deciding how to go about doing it" (Goodenough 1963: 258–259).

The above discussion focuses on the overarching concept of culture and its meaning. One may also speak of subcultures. Subcultures (sometimes called microcultures) are social groups that have clusters of behaviors, artifacts, values, and/or beliefs that are distinct from those of a larger cultural group, but the subculture is connected to the larger culture. The opening sentence of this essay contains several large cultures—American culture, Japanese culture, Egyptian culture—and examples of subcultures—geek culture, police culture, and so forth.

In more recent decades some anthropologists challenged the concept of culture as reflected in most of the definitions written prior to 1990. This was the period of what was termed "postmodernism." These critics felt that prior definitions were too rigid and implied that culture never changed and that it was homogeneous, that cultural elements were integrated and shared by all; they contended that the definitions were simplified and that culture as it was being defined did not exist. Some criticism focused more on how anthropologists study and gather cultural data and on the problems of doing objective ethnography. Such criticisms were really not new. I found throughout my career that thoughtful anthropologists always spoke about how difficult it is to agree on a single definition of culture and that not every member of a culture behaves the exact same way: There is quite a bit of variation within any culture; people in small homogeneous cultures share more cultural features than do members of large heterogeneous cultures; and culture is in a constant state of flux.

We all belong to a number of cultures—that of an ethnic group (e.g., Chicano, Anglo), that of an interest group (birdwatchers, online gamer), and so forth. And, while you may not dance the flamenco, if you are a Spaniard you know that it is a part of Spanish culture; if you are Mexican, you may not eat enchiladas but you know that this food is important in Mexican culture; if you are a Trobriand Islander, you may not grow yams or participate in yam distribution customs, but you know that this is part of Trobriand culture; you may not like or watch football, but if you are an American, you know that it is an important part of American culture. Culture is, as I am fond of telling students, what makes you a stranger when you are away from home. It is us.

As you read and contemplate the issues raised in the other essays in this book, I hope that you will recognize aspects of culture discussed here.

Challenge: Identify a behavior that is part of a culture or subculture to which you belong that you *do not* do yourself but that you recognize as part of that culture. Now identify a behavior of that culture that you *do* regularly.

Thinking It Through
- Discuss the development of the concept of culture in anthropology.
- Examine the difficulty of anthropologists agreeing on a single definition of culture.
- Identify the core features of the concept of culture.

Anthropological Terms

archaeology	ethnology
artifacts	feature
biological anthropology	holistic
cultural anthropology	linguistics
culture	participant observation
ethnography	

Thinking Practically
- Describe what you are wearing. How has your culture (or a subculture to which you belong) influenced your choice to wear these clothes—their color and fit, for example?
- Discuss a value that is shared within your culture (or a subculture to which you belong). Do all members demonstrate this value in their behavior?

2 ~ The 13-Letter Word

One rarely speaks of it and even your best friend will rarely tell you that it is showing, but ethnocentrism is a part of our lives and contributes to conflict and misunderstandings at home and around the world. This discussion underscores how enculturation provides the basis for our ethnocentrism.

While viewing a photograph of a Bedouin man with his several wives in a *National Geographic* magazine, a European woman comments, "Having several wives is disgusting and immoral." A Bedouin woman might remark, "How can those American women live without co-wives to share child rearing and work? They are surely lonely and stupid to insist on being the only wife." An American parent of European descent, visiting his child's elementary school, remarks, after asking directions from a young Cambodian immigrant, "I don't trust those Asian children. They never look at you when you speak to them." A recent Cambodian immigrant parent visiting the same school says, "American children show no respect to elders. They stare right in your eyes and tell you their opinion. This is wrong. I hope that my children don't become like them." These people are victims of their *ethnocentrism*.

Trained anthropologists sometimes discover the deep roots of ethnocentrism in themselves, too. Toward the completion of his first three years of fieldwork among the Ju/´hoansi (San people of the African Kalahari), anthropologist Richard Lee purchased the biggest, fattest ox he could find (from a neighboring group). The ox was to be a gift to the people in payment and appreciation for their cooperation. During the three years he lived with them, he had rarely shared food because his study focused on their food-gathering activities and he did not want to interfere with any of these activities. He knew they considered him to be stingy since he always had plenty of canned food to eat. When he gave them the ox, to his considerable dismay the Ju/'hoansi made unending, disparaging remarks about what a bag of bones the animal was and that it had no desirable fat on it and there would not be enough for everyone. He had expected people to be grateful for this gift. After the animal was butchered it was obvious that the ox was filled with fat and everyone had a wonderful time at the feast he gave. Puzzled and agitated, Lee later spoke with several Ju/'hoansi men and asked why they had said all of those disparaging things about the ox. It was explained to him that one always insulted hunters this way when they were successful, otherwise they would become arrogant. This was a way to enforce humility. For all the time he was with them, he had missed this key custom and the value behind it. Lee had been ethnocentric—giving a fine gift was the right way to say thank you. The Ju/'hoansi had been ethnocentric, too, because they held that their value of enforcing humility in hunters (or someone who provided a big, fat ox) was the right way to treat people.

Listen carefully to people around you and in the media everyday. For example, you overhear a group of people discussing religion—one advocating a Christian perspective on an issue, while another presenting a view held by a Hindu, or someone supporting the Islamic faith, or perhaps an atheist expressing her opinions. While each may outwardly maintain a politically correct position on the issue while in public, you know from reading the letters to the editor in your local paper that some, perhaps even most, are thinking that the views of the others are just not right and that their belief system is the true one. Comparisons of values are usually based on one's own cultural or subcultural upbringing in matters of faith and belief. Your pastor, priest, rabbi, or imam may urge acceptance of others' beliefs. If, however, there is a small voice within you that compares the values of another group to your own, and you *know* that your view is the correct view, you are being ethnocentric.

Ethnocentrism is an own-group-centered attitude. Being ethnocentric is making a value judgment about another *culture*, subculture, or microculture based on one's own cultural (or subcultural, or microcultural) views, behaviors, ways of thinking, values, or beliefs. Note: Do not confuse this with *egocentrism*, which is a judgment that is based on a personal, individual belief. Ethnocentrism is the cultural disease that we all share. It is socially transmitted. People rarely speak of it, and even your best friend usually won't tell you that it is showing. Symptoms of ethnocentrism can appear at any time but are most apparent when traveling in another country; surfing the web; watching a TV sitcom; watching, listening to, or reading about events in the news; and discussing world or local issues. Topics that bring it to the surface most quickly include behaviors, values, religion, and *ethnicity*. Ethnocentrism may ruin your holiday; it may also affect or ruin business dealings and potential friendships. If you pay attention, you can identify when you are being ethnocentric; you can also identify when other people are being ethnocentric. Yet, we Americans rarely identify, as ethnocentrism, behaviors such as a US-based NGO going to Africa or elsewhere to implement programs that aim to change the others' culture—to believe, behave, and think as we do. Native members of other world cultures often recognize this as American ethnocentrism. The opposite of ethnocentrism is *cultural relativism*, an approach that views and evaluates aspects of a culture only within the context of that culture.

While on a recent trip along the California coast to observe elephant seals calving, I observed two examples of ethnocentrism. First, I overheard a foreign tourist remark to her companion, in Spanish, that Americans were stupid to get so excited about protecting a bunch of seals. Later, my husband and I chatted for some time to a park docent who shared details about the life history of the elephant seals. Rapport was established as we learned that she, too, had been a teacher. We compared notes about teaching and the state of education in California and how state budget cuts

11

were impacting schools. Then I asked her if they had many foreign visitors to this location. She paused, looking thoughtful, and then said, "Yes, but most of them should stay home." Somewhat surprised but attributing her candor to the rapport we had established, I asked why she felt that way. She elaborated that the foreigners broke rules regularly, such as parking their cars in inappropriate places. They did not stay behind barriers that prevented beach access and that were erected to protect both the seals and the public; furthermore, she said that they broke rules much more often than Americans. She also said that they were arrogant and rude.

She told of one French family who actually used wire cutters to cut through a fence in order to get closer to the seals on the beach. She and another docent told them to stop or the docents would be forced to call the police, as the tourists were endangering both themselves and the seals. These tourists cursed and made disparaging remarks about America and Americans and their "stupid" rules, in both French (which our docent spoke) and English. She further stated that German tourists were only marginally better than the French. She said that when she began being a docent she thought she just had bad luck encountering a few such visitors. After doing this volunteer work for five years, she no longer thought it was just a few foreign tourists; instead it was common behavior of people from those countries, at least those who traveled. She stated that she thought it was part of their culture to be rude and disrespectful of authority. She said that American tourists behaved better. She was making a statement about the French and German tourists based on her American values of how one should behave in this setting. She was making value judgments. She was being ethnocentric. She could have made a statement to me without a value judgment such as: "The French apparently have different attitudes about how to behave in state preserves such as this." She might go on to say how she had observed them behaving, but again without making a value judgment based on American culture.

Clearly, these French tourists and visitors of other nationalities were being ethnocentric, too. Rather than merely noting differences in behaviors, such as saying, "It's interesting that Americans post rules about how close to get to the seals, rather than, "Americans are weird in that they treat animals as if they had feelings; our getting closer to them to take a photograph won't bother them." Anyone who has experienced living in another culture can give examples of values and behaviors that are shared by most members of that culture but are different than those of American culture. Of course not all French or all Americans think and behave alike. In our large heterogeneous societies today, there are many subcultural groups, and people within one subculture can be ethnocentric by making judgmental comparisons with other subcultural groups.

The docent's final remark was that she just didn't get it. Why did foreigners come here if they felt so negative about America and our way of life? As we drove away, my husband and I discussed her comments. Her ethnocentrism in this situation is somewhat understandable. Her society, American, was being verbally attacked, and she was judging the visitors from her culture's view of what was rude and what was appropriate behavior in a park setting like the elephant seal preserve. Were the French nationals doing the same? Should it be a requirement of foreign travel to have an understanding of the issue of ethnocentrism and how it can impact international relations?

A neighbor of mine hosted a German exchange student several years ago. Two months into the visit she told me that she and her son would be happy when the semester was over. On weekends they had taken the young man to historic places, shown him around, and taken him to Disneyland. She said he was always saying that Germany did things better, that the German people were more intelligent, and he constantly made disparaging, judgmental comments about Americans. She allowed that he was perhaps homesick, but it gave her and her family nothing but negative feelings about him specifically and Germany in general. As we talked, I realized her feelings stemmed from how the student said things, always with a negative judgmental comparison between the two cultures. Instead he could have simply stated that he found it interesting that Americans did some things quite differently than Germans. I've been told similar stories from other exchange-student hosts, but I've also heard wonderfully

13

positive stories from hosts about their exchange-student experiences when the visiting student was open to exploring what Americans had to offer and didn't note cultural differences in a negative, ethnocentric way. I've wondered what host families in other countries experience from foreign exchange students, including Americans. I do know from personal experience and observations while living in Spain that some American tourists can be quite ethnocentric and vocal when expressing their view. The ethnocentrism was not appreciated in the village where I lived.

My point in sharing these examples is that ethnocentrism projected by a few individuals can affect how others feel about the larger cultural group. The process of *enculturation*, learning one's culture by growing up in it, is at the core of ethnocentrism. I hear my five-year-old grandson repeating values he is learning—be kind to others, try hard and practice your soccer skills, work hard, be an individual—and I think of five-year-olds in other communities—Trobriand, Ya̧nomamö, French, Indonesian, for example, and the values that they are learning by the same process. I just read him a book about a stray cat that chases other cats and kittens (*The Fire Cat* by Esther Averill). My grandson remarked that the cat is being a bully, a topic often discussed in schools and around American dinner tables. A lady befriends the cat in the story and gives him food. One day he has to be rescued because he climbed too high up in a tree, it is rainy and windy, and he is too frightened to come down. The firemen come and rescue him and invite the cat to live with them in the fire station. He likes it at the fire station and decides to learn to help the firemen. The fire chief tells the cat that it is good that he can do jobs to help the firemen but he must also be kind to other cats and not chase them away from the station. The cat gradually starts being nice to other cats, and one day, when a call comes into the station about a kitten stuck in a tall tree, he accompanies the firemen to the location. There it is discovered that the cat is high up on a small branch, the fire ladder can't reach so far, and the branch won't support a fireman. The firehouse cat climbs the ladder, jumps onto the branch, talks to the little cat, picks it up gently in his mouth the way a mother cat would, and carries it to safety. The fire chief rewards the cat by giving him a small fire hat and making him the official firehouse cat. My grandson tells me that it is really good that the cat has learned to be kind. Such children's books and oral tales are part of reinforcement and enculturation in every culture, and they reflect that culture's core values. Of course, children also observe and listen to adults around them and internalize what they see and hear.

Napoleon Chagnon in his classic ethnography of the Yąnomamö Indians of Brazil and Venezuela narrates a scene in his film, *The Ax Fight*, that illustrates part of the enculturation of Yąnomamö youth: The camera focuses on a group of children, both boys and girls. The boys are holding long clubs (like those used by their elders during confrontations and fights) and moving menacingly toward little girls. Chagnon says something to the effect that among the Yąnomamö little boys intimidate little girls. The children's behavior is reinforcing their learned cultural view about gender roles and fierceness. Boys are enculturated to be fierce, not kind. Most Americans would feel ethnocentric about this.

It is an interesting personal exercise to attempt to identify your own ethnocentrisms. This does not mean you should change your own group-centered values or behaviors. By identifying your ethnocentric reactions, however, you may become more empathetic about where others are "coming from." With the recognition that all peoples have the affliction of ethnocentrism, you expose the roots of misunderstandings and conflict. Such recognition gives perspective. I have to admit that even with my background and training in the anthropological perspective, on occasion I find myself saying, "Oops, that was an ethnocentric thought."

Use anthropology every day by being aware of ethnocentrism, both yours and others'. Drawing attention to how culture instills our ethnocentric attitudes is, in a broad sense, what anthropology has always been about. Education and awareness of ethnocentrism can help all of us to be more thoughtful about our attitudes toward people of other cultural backgrounds.

Challenge: Might it be argued that some worldwide humanitarian efforts by American NGOs are fueled by ethnocentrism?

15

Thinking It Through
- Examine the concept of ethnocentrism.
- Identify how people everywhere acquire it as part of the enculturation process.
- Delineate how ethnocentrism impacts everyday life.

Anthropological Terms

cultural relativism	enculturation
culture	ethnicity
egocentrism	ethnocentrism

Thinking Practically
- Pay attention when you are traveling or in a new cultural (subcultural or microcultural) setting. Can you identify your ethnocentric thoughts?
- Describe two ways that ethnocentrism could negatively impact business relationships between two cultures.

3 ~ Does Anyone Here Speak English?

The role of learning and using a local language as a means for establishing rapport while conducting participant observation is explored, as well as using local languages during tourist encounters.

"How much is this in real money and does anyone here speak English?" Words that made me cringe as I stood at the back of the small tourist shop in the medieval village of Santillana del Mar in Cantabria, Spain. The tone of the speaker, whom I recognized immediately as an American, based on her pronunciation, was harsh and demanding. The shop owner explained in slow careful Spanish that she could only accept the local currency and that the nearby bank was closing in minutes for the siesta period.

When the tourist began again, this time complaining about the local custom of the afternoon closure of shops, businesses, and schools, I could stand it no longer. I moved to the front of the shop and, in my less-than-perfect but serviceable Spanish, apologized for my fellow countrywoman. I then turned to the tourist and as politely as I could, translated what the clerk had said. The woman left the shop in a huff while muttering to herself. The clerk breathed a sigh of relief and thanked me. We chatted a bit about the difficulties of travel, though it was no excuse for a foreign visitor to be so rude.

When traveling, a person has the unique opportunity to be a *participant observer* and learn about another people and their culture. Alas, *ethnocentrism* often rears its ugly head in tourist encounters. And, I submit that refusal to at least *try* to communicate in the local language is a component of an ethnocentric attitude—an own-group-centered attitude, in this case a culture.

A basic tenant of cultural anthropology is that it is important to *establish rapport* with people if you want to learn from them while doing *fieldwork*, including *participant observation*. In the long history of anthropological fieldwork, learning to speak to people in their own language, or at least attempting to do so, is an important way to know more about them—skill in communication is an valuable tool. Many of the earlier generations of anthropologists spent a year or more with their study group learning the language. They did this while carrying out basic activities like mapping the area, taking a basic census, describing daily activities, and getting acquainted with local people before they conducted detailed interviews. Anthropologist Bruce Knauft, for example, in recounting his fieldwork experiences with the Gebusi of Papua New Guinea, notes that he knew that learning the language of the Gebusi would be his biggest challenge. He and his wife, Eileen, had been trained in how to learn an unwritten language when translators were unavailable. Still, it took them over six months with the help of an interested Gebusi named Yuway to learn even the basics of the complexities of Gebusi grammar. For example, this language emphasizes verbs and often leaves out nouns and descriptive phrases. Today, there are language guides and even courses that one can take to learn most of the world's languages prior to fieldwork. More than 6,800 spoken languages have been studied and grammars and dictionaries written for many of them (often by *linguistic anthropologists*).

Think about it. If an anthropologist is really interested in what a man calls his mother's brother's son or why a ritual is performed before planting crops, it stands to reason that the person being interviewed might believe the genuineness of interest if the anthropologist takes the trouble to learn and converse in the local language. Of course, learning a new language takes time and you don't want to misinterpret what is said. For these reasons diplomats, businesspeople, travelers, and even anthropologists often utilize the services of translators if they are available—at least until they become confident in the new language.

Even as a tourist *genuine* interest in local people, their history, and contemporary culture is communicated if you speak their language. Speak less than perfectly? Have to ask for help? Good. These "deficiencies" show your human side and will usually help foster rapport. Bruce Knauft reported that the people joined him and his wife in laughing at their many mistakes. Shared laughter helps establish rapport.

There is an additional plus to learning a language. There are words or phrases that simply don't translate directly from one language to another. A facsimile of a word can be given but nuance and cultural content often can't. It was a lesson that my family learned repeatedly in Spain. A Spanish *paseo* isn't just a "walk" as English speakers use the word. It is more a "stroll" or "ramble" that is usually done socially with others. Ask someone who has lived in Spain. Furthermore, there is a sticky linguistic issue famously hypothesized in the **Sapir-Whorf hypothesis** (developed by two early anthropological linguists). Simply stated, these researchers suggested that a person's language forms his or her reality. Much debate has resulted from this idea. The Nuer herders of East Africa, for example, have multiple words for their cattle. They use hundreds of single words to identify cattle types by configurations of their horns and their hide colors, patterns of color, and color combinations. Does this mean the Nuer "see" cattle differently than Americans who have very few words for types of cattle? Recent linguistic work suggests that a rich vocabulary simply gives a person more detail. But the debate continues on whether verbs and the structure of language affect the way people view their world. For example, if a language does not have a past or future verb tense, do speakers of that language reside more in the present? It is an interesting idea to ponder.

The importance of using the local language was brought to focus for me when my family and I lived in a village of 1,500 people in northern

Spain. Following good anthropological tradition, we always spoke Spanish, or tried to. Our Spanish was far from perfect, learned in high school and university courses. We taught our daughter, then nine, basic phrases and brushed up on our vocabulary before embarking on our journey. It amazed us how the locals seemed to appreciate our efforts. From local shop owners to our landlord, everyone wanted to help us improve our Spanish. On our first evening in the village we were in a small stationery and school-supply store making purchases. My daughter and I made some remark about "*mi esposo*" (my husband) meeting us in the square in a few minutes. The young son (also nine years old) of the proprietor immediately remarked "*Ah no, no, es tu marido, no es tu esposo.*" Further discussion revealed that "esposo" (from the verb *esposar*—to handcuff) was used in Mexico (we'd learned our Spanish in California), and in Cantabrian Spain the terms *marido* (husband) and *mujer* (woman) are used for husband and wife. Our language lessons had begun and continued throughout our stay. We apologized for our ignorance and told them that we welcomed their assistance because we would be living in their community for some time.

Over the months that followed we had many conversations with locals that led to them, on learning of our nationality (they saw few Americans), complaining bitterly about the usual visitors to this area who wouldn't even attempt to say common words and phrases in Spanish. As our friend Paco remarked (in Spanish of course), "Those Germans, or French, or Dutch, or British tourists all act so superior." When we asked for elaboration Paco replied, "They will only speak German, or French, or English. They don't even try basic words or phrases. They are in our country but they aren't really interested in us as people." We heard similar complaints often.

One day while eagerly awaiting the birth of a calf in the barn at the small dairy farm of a new friend of our daughter, we heard it again. The farmer, after a protracted explanation of the artificial insemination of this particular cow and the pedigrees of the bull (some of which we did not follow in its entirety, I must admit) said: "You aren't German are you?"

"No," we replied, "North Americans." He then said, "I didn't think you could be Germans, although you are tall, because those Germans won't even ask for bread in the store or say good morning or thank you in Spanish." This statement was delivered there, in that fragrant barn by this weather-faced man of the soil, with a great deal of disgust and animation. Then he elaborated on this theme as others had done. He ended by telling us to come for a visit any time. Of course we know that other issues may well have influenced this man's attitude toward Germans—politics and history in particular—but the language issue of visiting tourists certainly pushed a button for him.

I've said that we spoke Spanish exclusively when interacting with local people when we lived in Spain. Yet, this was quite taxing during the first months so we usually spoke English when alone in our flat. Because all media and interpersonal communications with shop owners were in Spanish we essentially experienced immersion in the language outside of our flat. OK, I'll admit that we once traveled by bus to the nearest large city, the provincial capital, with the express desire of finding something to read in English. There we found a copy of the *International Herald Tribune*—published only in English. After searching three bookstores, we found two novels in English. On another occasion I actually spent one morning stalking tourists in the village until I heard them speak. If they spoke English (usually they were British tourists on their way to southern Spain), I introduced myself, told them a little about my anthropological fieldwork experience in the town, and literally begged them to sell me any novels that they had with them that they'd finished. I managed to acquire several books in this manner, though most people took pity on me and gave me the books.

After dinner, we took turns reading these books aloud. Reading in our native language helped to alleviate the stresses of always trying to use the correct verb tense in Spanish (in particular we had difficulty with the subjunctive) and feeling dumb because we didn't have a more expansive vocabulary.

For us, except for our withdrawal to read books in English, immersion worked. Our daughter began speaking correctly accented and grammatically correct Spanish quickly with the help of other children and adults. My husband and I got progressively better as the weeks passed. *It was survival.* We do not require immigrants to the United States to learn English as part of the **acculturation** process. Acculturation is the process of acquiring a culture that is different from one's birth culture as a consequence of prolonged contact with that culture. In my state alone, the official *California Voters Guide* is offered in seven languages. The *California Driver Handbook* is offered in nine languages. Businesses, medical practices, and other professional groups advertise that they speak Spanish, Portuguese, Mandarin, Hindi, Arabic, and other languages. I know that this is a very complex issue, but I have wondered if some of the politically strong views about immigration might be caused by the *perception* by citizens and native English speakers that new arrivals seemingly don't *try*.

My family talked often, on our return to the United States, about how many doors had been opened to us by these friendly and generous people in Spain because we respected them enough to communicate, however inexpertly, in their language. What depth it gave to our experiences—besides seeing the beautiful country, the castles, the Upper Paleolithic caves, and the cathedrals—to talk with people. I remember Paco commenting to us one day that he knew speaking another language is difficult (he by the way speaks Portuguese, French, and German in addition to his native Spanish), but it is the *trying* that counted with him. He also said that he thought that our actions contributed to international goodwill. I believe that this is something for tourists to consider.

Oh yes, the calf was finally born, a healthy female. She was, to my great surprise, given the name "Roberta."

Challenge: How do you feel when you encounter someone in your community who doesn't try to communicate with you or a store clerk in English?

Thinking It Through
- Discuss language as a tool for establishing rapport while conducting fieldwork or traveling.

- Examine how communicating in the language of the host country contributes to more meaningful tourist encounters.

Anthropological Terms

acculturation	linguistic anthropologist
establish rapport	participant observer
ethnocentrism	participant observation
fieldwork	Sapir-Whorf hypothesis

Thinking Practically

- Discuss how the tourist experience can be a form of participant observation, with learning some of the native language as part of establishing rapport.
- Find more information about the Sapir-Whorf hypothesis and apply this idea to an English-only tourist experience versus an experience where you try to utilize the local language.
- Should there be strict adherence to the use of English-only for commercial and business transactions in the United States? Defend your answer.

4 ~ A Long and Boring Day

A key method used by anthropologists while conducting ethno-
graphic fieldwork, participant observation is considered within
the context of the author undergoing Mohs surgery (used in the
treatment of skin cancer). The approach of participant obser-
vation within this setting underscores how an insider's view
(emic approach) adds to the description of an event and pro-
vides an additional perspective on traditional interviews.

Yuck. 10:30 AM. Here we sit, seven of us with bandages on various parts of our faces—two on noses, one on a forehead, and four on cheeks (including me). I've been here three and a half hours, and counting, as have the others. No, we aren't survivors of a passing hurricane or tornado or auto accident. We are all in various phases of Mohs surgery to remove skin cancers.

I approached this as another occasion to be a ***participant observer***. Really, even though I suppose it sounds a bit ghoulish, I've found this approach to work well in taking my mind off of an unpleasant situation. Everyone in the waiting room has a form of skin cancer, mostly basal cell cancers thought to be caused by sun damage (UVA and UVB rays). Mohs surgery—where cells are removed one layer at a time until laboratory pathology reports show no more cancer cells—has a 97–98 percent success rate with no reoccurrence.

Participant observation is an important component of ethnographic research. By not only observing events and activities but also *participating*, one gets to feel the experience and record an assessment of what is happening from that perspective. An ethnographer rarely gets to be a full participant. For example, Napoleon Chagnon was primarily an observer (a spectator) and documenter of the *culture* of the Yąnomamö Indians of Brazil and Venezuela. This was particularly true of his first time in the field. He carried out his ethnographic study during an initial 15-month period, followed by additional months spanning three decades. He gradually learned the language, began to interview tribe members, and spoke with them informally; he sampled their foods and learned many customs such as the proper greeting when entering a new *shabano* (village). He observed events such as chest-pounding duels, wife beating, and intervillage warfare (conflict between different *shabanos*). He did not, however, participate in most Yąnomamö activities—such as confrontations called club fights, where participants wielded long poles used to intimidate one another.

Over time, as Chagnon became better known to the people, he had opportunities to participate. In one reported incident he asked a shaman whom he had come to know well, *and whom he called "friend,"* to perform a curing ceremony on him. In another, he took hallucinogenic drugs with them. Yąnomamö males use hallucinogens to get in touch with spirits and the spirit universe. During his first few field trips Chagnon described the plant materials that the Yąnomamö collected, how they extracted the part containing the drug, how they prepared and took it—the latter by having a friend blow the drug powder, mixed with ashes, up their nostrils. They always invited him to join them. He reported that he thought it unethical to participate in this activity. He continued to refuse to participate until very late in his fieldwork when he decided he would participate once in order to discover and describe his feelings while under the influence of the drug, hoping it would give him more insight into the Yąnomamö. Few anthropologists become immersed in a culture for as long as Chagnon. On later fieldwork visits, he was able to share his ethnographic data with the Yąnomamö themselves, and they discussed his perceptions compared to their own regarding events. In other words, they talked together about culture and worldview, making his *ethnogra-*

26

phy more complete in showing both the view of an insider (called the *emic* view) and that of an outside observer (called the *etic* view).

I was going to be a full participant in this morning's activities. Although I was not collecting data over days, months, or years, my observations, descriptions, and feelings could contribute to knowledge about this procedure as viewed from a patient's perspective. If I were working for a consulting firm I would follow through with observing numerous procedures (with permission) and interview medical staff and patients. The professional ethics in such *applied research* require transparency and full disclosures to everyone involved.

In this *microculture* (in this case, a medical clinic exclusively dedicated to carrying out Mohs surgery; a single-day patient immersion experience) I begin, as ethnographers often do, with observing and describing the site. The doctor's office is in a complex of offices occupied by other medical offices. The waiting room is small, approximately 15 by 20 feet. It is carpeted in a beige-tone carpet and the walls are painted in an off-white color. The furniture consists of eight overstuffed chairs covered in light-brown imitation leather. The eight chairs are arranged along two adjacent walls. They bracket a corner table with a lamp and various current magazines on it. A small table in the opposite corner holds more magazines, a coffee pot, and a large box of doughnuts. The wall next to this table has a window open to a receptionist's desk. A few simple decorations are on the walls—framed botanical leaf and flower prints. If I were conducting a larger research study I would visit this office often as well as visit other such clinics. Data collected would be compared with the hope of revealing cultural themes. For example, do all such offices offer coffee and doughnuts to patients? The receptionist is a pleasant-speaking young woman in her 30s. She smiled when asking my name and taking my medical insurance information. As I finish jotting this description, a woman wearing a light green uniform opens an interior door and calls my name.

It begins. The surgical room contains just a padded chair that reminds me of a large, leather, home-style recliner without arms that can be reclined to a flat position. There is a bright, large (ca 20 inches in diameter) light hanging above the recliner; a small stainless steel cart with instruments is adjacent to the recliner; and a sink and shelf is along one wall. As I take note of the room the surgical nurse is explaining the procedure and smiling and speaking in a cheerful voice. I consider that she is trying to be reassuring and put me at ease. At ease? I think, hmm; I wonder if she thinks anyone can be relaxed in these circumstances. I do know this is a highly treatable form of cancer (what a fear-filled word in our culture) and the doctor has an excellent reputation. But really, it is difficult to be fully relaxed and at ease. I contemplate whether other patients feel at ease and reflect that a question about how a patient feels, as the procedure begins, would be a good question for interviews. It is considered a good interview technique to formulate interview questions based on what is important to the people in the research situation rather than entering the study with prepared questions. Detailed pre-prepared questions may reflect researcher bias, and this may not be what members of the study group feel is important.

The doctor enters and asks a few questions, tells me to always use sunscreen, and explains that this will be a long and boring day. He describes what he will do—cells are removed (read "scraped") from the site on the face using special instruments after the site is deadened with an injection of an anesthetic. Any blood vessels that are severed are sealed by electrical burning. Are you still with me? Then the removed tissue is prepared on slides and examined in the on-site laboratory. During this time the site on my face will be covered with gauze and a bandage and I will return to the waiting room to, well, wait. Results are known in 30–60 minutes. If the area is not clear, the procedure is repeated as many times as necessary.

Before the procedure begins, I attempt to engage the doctor a bit by asking if he had a pleasant holiday. Establishing a bit of rapport (an important ethnographic technique) can't hurt. He replies "yes," but it is clear from his short response and failure to ask me the same question, that he does not want to engage in a conversation. I try again later, but without result. He is working and I am just another patient needing his medical expertise. Rather than worry about what he is doing I try to again think like someone immersed in participant observation. For one thing, I consider what this experience could teach me about contemporary medical practice if I were working for an applied anthropology firm that was hired to analyze how services could be improved. Knowing that there are many anthropologists today engaged in consulting for businesses, government agencies, and NGOs, I decide that this analysis is worthwhile. Of course, applied anthropological researchers in a medical facility do more observations and interviewing than the *immersion participant observation* that I am doing.

Instruments clink, and I feel a little pinch-sting as the anesthetic medication is administered with a syringe. The doctor says he will be right back and leaves the room. The nurse says the anesthetic should take effect immediately. She is chipper and smiles a lot. She addresses me as "Miss Roberta." The doctor asked me how to pronounce my last name when he first arrived and since has called me "Sweetie." I presume this is what he calls all women older than he. The feminist in me wants to protest the use of this term and to ask if he calls his male patients "sweetie," "big guy," or "sir." However, I remind myself that I'm being a participant observer, and such an exchange does not seem prudent when he will soon wield a scalpel on my face.

The doctor returns, tells me to position my head to the side, and begins. I feel a little tug and hear several zaps of the electrical instrument sealing exposed blood vessels, and then it is done. No pain at all. The doctor again says, "Now begins a long boring day," on his way out the door, taking removed tissue to the lab. The nurse places a temporary gauze-and-tape cover on the wound, and I'm told to return to the waiting room.

The demeanor of the other patients in the waiting room, three women and three men, all of whom I estimate to be over 50, is somber, as is that of their support persons. Blank faces. No one is making eye contact. No one looks at anyone else's gauzed face. There is little talking, and communication is always in hushed tones. Have these people been enculturated that this is appropriate behavior under these circumstances? Are they frightened? More observation and interviews would reveal data on this. Since I am a member of the same culture, however, I know that I've been taught that this demeanor is one of respect for others' privacy. I am not frightened but admit to being under some stress.

I have come equipped to spend the day (I was told to do this when the appointment was made) as have other patients in the waiting room. I have lunch and snacks, a bag containing the knit hat that I'm making for my grandson, a magazine, and a novel. As I sit down, I smile at the woman in the chair next to mine, who has gauze and tape on the tip of her nose, and she smiles back. My husband, who insisted on accompanying me this morning "for moral support," asks how I'm doing. I whisper that I'm fine and this really isn't a big deal.

Then in a normal voice I remark, "I sure wish I'd been told as a teenager in Southern California that lying on the beaches for hours in pursuit of the perfect tan might lead to this." The woman next to me comments that she did that too and even slathered baby oil on her skin. I recall that my friends and I all believed that baby oil would give us a great tan. We did use a famous brand of tanning oil too—it was advertised on billboards that showed a beach with a cute small child displaying a lovely tan. You could tell that the child was tan because a little dog was pulling down a corner of her panties revealing white skin. Alas, we were to learn too late that these early suntan oil formulas did not block both UVA and UVB rays. The UVB light (B-range ultraviolet radiation) penetrates to the bottom layers of skin cells and causes the sun damage leading to skin cancer on the surface of the skin.

Other patients begin to chime in now that my neighbor and I are talking. They share remarks about their own sun experiences and the fact that everyone wanted a tan and the dangers of too much sun exposure were never mentioned at home or in the media. One elderly gentleman comments that he always worked around his family farm shirtless. He says that this is his third visit to this clinic. Someone else says she doesn't understand why people use tanning booths, given the risks of ending up here, especially when one can use spray tanning.

The anthropological voice inside my head shouts "Culture, culture, culture!" Clearly, as you know, culture consists of accumulated, shared knowledge, and behaviors of a social group that are learned as one grows up. Today, medical knowledge has added to our understanding of the damage that can be done by the sun. Yet, many people still lie out in the sun or go to tanning salons. My 35-year-old friend, a natural blond like me with lightly pigmented skin and blue eyes, is a devotee of tanning and has already had several basal cells removed from her back. She's heard the message but loves the look of a real suntan; she says that she feels more attractive and sexy and thinks that spray tans look fake.

Biological anthropologist Nina Jablonski and her husband George Chaplin have researched and written extensively about human skin. They suggest that skin cancers are primarily a consequence of human migrations, past and contemporary, that result in "mismatches between skin pigmentation and geography or lifestyle" (2010: 8963).

They present molecular evidence for how and why natural selection operated to select for human skin color pigments over the course of more than five million years of human evolution. They explain how dark skin pigmentation is adaptive in equatorial regions where concentrations of ultraviolet sunlight rays known as UVA and UVB are highest. A vitamin known as vitamin D3 is synthesized in human skin when the skin is exposed to sunlight. The amount of color pigmentation in the skin cells affects the process of vitamin D3 synthesis. The role of vitamin D3 in bodily development and health are complex. For example, vitamin D3 is essential to healthy skeletal bone development. Dark pigmentation protects against the toxic effects of too much vitamin D3. It protects against cell damage that leads to skin cancer. Light skin pigmentation provides advantages to people who live in northern latitudes—lightly pigmented skin allows for *sufficient* amounts of vitamin D3 to synthesize in these areas where there is less annual sunlight.

The research demonstrates that light-skinned people are especially at risk for UV damage to skin when they live in, say, Southern California, as I did (latitude 34° 3′N), while my ancestors all came from far northern

31

Europe (latitude 56° 29′ N) where for generations light skin was selected for. Does this evolutionary knowledge together with an appreciation of the role of cultural values and the *enculturation* process comfort me? At an intellectual level it does, as it tells me that my cancer is not my fault. Science in my youth had incomplete knowledge of the impact of sun exposure to individuals of various skin pigmentations.

My musing is interrupted by another call into surgery. I won't bore the reader with additional descriptions of the procedures. Suffice it to say that I got the all clear with the third episode, followed by the doctor suturing and bandaging the wound. After five-and-a-half hours I bid the other waiting patients good luck as I exited the office. My anthropological lens, using participant observation helped pass the time.

What would I write up in my report about my observations and participation if I were working for a consulting firm? (Of course, more time would be spent observing in this and other clinics; there would be interviews with both patients and doctors; and comparative analyses [including quantitative analysis where possible] would be carried out.) In my report of this particular day's participant observation, I would note to congratulate the doctor and nurse for their diligent protocols for hand washing before each encounter with my face, plus wearing latex gloves. I would suggest that more information of an educational nature be directed at patients *before* their procedures. This could be accomplished with a hand-out sheet or booklet or being directed to an internet website. For example, I experienced a rapid heartbeat and tremors after the administration of the anesthetic. When I voiced this, I was told, "Oh, that is a common response to the epinephrine in the anesthetic." Hmm. Well, it was a tad scary while it lasted (I dropped two knitting stitches while sitting in the waiting room between procedures). I would emphasize that although the office routine was an often repeated routine for the staff, they should be reminded that each *new patient* is experiencing it for the first (and hopefully last) time, and that verbal reassurance as the hours pass might alleviate some stress. I'm not certain I'd mention the "Sweetie" issue.

Challenge: Observe advertisements in a variety of media formats: What *nonverbal* messages do they give about playing out in the sun? In what ways are people with lightly pigmented skin encouraged to tan? Where individuals are in a location with significant sun exposure, is there any indication that UVA/UVB exposure is being curtailed, perhaps with clothing or a hat, and if so, how does this advertisement compare with one that is promoting the use of a UVA/UVB sunscreen?

Thinking It Through

- Describe the fieldwork method of participant observation and show how this approach can add a dimension to a person's everyday experiences.
- Explain how participant observation can aid applied anthropologists in uncovering insights that may not be found in questionnaires or one-time interviews.
- Explain how these insights may aid in the development of programs in institutions and business.

Anthropological Terms

culture	immersion participant observation
emic	microculture
enculturation	participant observation
ethnography	participant observer
etic	

Thinking Practically

- Discuss how and why perceptions may differ for an ethnographer who only *observes* behaviors from one who actually *participates* in a behavior within the culture being studied.
- Some sun exposure has been demonstrated to be necessary for your skin to synthesize vitamin D3. If a person has lightly pigmented skin, lives in northern latitudes, always covers exposed skin with a sunblock product, and spends most of his or her daytime hours indoors, discuss how this may affect the person's future health given our current state of knowledge.

5 ~ The Hospital as Foreign Culture

This essay observes the local hospital as a foreign culture, as the author accompanies her husband who is having minor surgery. The experience provides an opportunity to look at a microculture and explore some ethnographic fieldwork methods including establishing rapport and identifying ideal and actual cultural behaviors. The difficulty of coping with culture shock is also addressed.

It was 7:00 AM. The staff was being efficient—asking questions, filling out admission forms, following pre-op protocol. We had entered a foreign *culture* or what anthropologists call a ***microculture*** (a small culture subset within a culture where a group of people share a cluster of learned behaviors, beliefs, and knowledge not shared by other members of the larger culture). We knew of this microculture within our society and had something of a glimpse into the behavior of its inhabitants from popular television programs and comments from friends who had "visited" this culture previously. We'd heard from these sources some of the specialized, shared language and vocabulary of the hospital staff—pre-op, post-op, ICA, CCU, DNR, IV, but this knowledge did not prepare us to be a participant in the culture any more than knowing words like *gracias, por favor, frijole, jefe,* or *mercado* prepared us to participate in life in Spain, except in the most peripheral way.

I was the wife of a man facing surgery. My role was to be his support during this experience. I decided to use my anthropological lenses and ethnographic background to observe this microculture. It would help the waiting and worrying time pass. Making careful observations in unfamiliar cultural settings, both foreign and at home, is a foundation of *participant observation*, one method of data gathering in cultural anthropology.

When in a new cultural environment, the anthropologist first typically observes the environment and the people in it rather like a "fly on the wall." The goal of these early observations is to get one's bearings and note what behaviors may be a focal point of the culture; this form of observation also helps to determine what questions to ask of the natives and to whom one might best direct those questions. Additionally, this observation period allows one to work on acquiring language fluency. In the case of the hospital microculture, we spoke the same language as the natives, yet we did not commonly utilize many of the vocabulary terms that they regularly employ. We asked many questions, and from my reading of the body language and responses given, we felt even more uncomfortable. I wondered if extensive questioning by patients was not a usual, expected behavior in this microculture. The natives were in charge and we were expected to just go along.

This place, the hospital, as with most cultural environments, was designed by the natives to serve them and facilitate the tasks they perform here. The staff member at the admission desk and the intake nurse are the first natives we encounter. This is the day prior to the actual surgery. The woman at admissions asks a number of questions. She often makes eye contact with my husband during this process but only looks at me, sitting at his side, twice. She explains the forms that she is filling out on her computer, and when the forms are completed, she prints them out. After my husband signs the forms, we are given a copy.

This worker is being professional, doing the job. I decide to try to *establish rapport* (a standard ethnographic technique) with her. I comment, "You look so wide-awake, when did your shift begin?" She smiles and replies, "At 6:00 AM." She then says that she does well until around 10:00 AM and then feels tired. She additionally notes that she is glad that she works only eight-hour shifts, unlike many at the hospital who work

12-hour shifts. After a few more pleasant exchanges we are directed to go down the hall to the pre-op area. We are told to follow the yellow line on the floor. There is also a blue line and a red line parallel to the yellow line. No signs (that we are able to observe) indicate where each line goes. Natives know and apparently it is part of their job to tell patients and visitors which line to follow. I actually have a momentary thought to *follow the yellow brick road* and consider that Dorothy probably experienced **culture shock** (see below) during her adventure in Oz.

The yellow line extends down a hallway that leads from the main room of the hospital; this room is called the lobby. The furniture in the lobby consists of several overstuffed sofas and chairs covered in a patterned fabric. They are a bit shabby and covered with dark spots. Several people are in the lobby sitting, including one young child who is coughing. My husband remarks that such fixtures seem at odds with the hospital's pledge to be a clean environment. Following the yellow line down the hall toward the pre-op area we note several other hallways branching from this main hall, down one of them the red line continues and the blue line goes down another. There are many closed doors along the hallway. There are no markings on these doors. We also pass an elevator. It is quiet. We only see one person walking ahead of us. The floors are highly polished linoleum in an off-white color. We continue following the yellow line.

We arrive at the pre-op area. We have seen employees in several different types of dress. I assume they represent people who do different jobs, and I pledge to look more closely at the name tags that each wears to see if this is true; perhaps clothing type is significant in this microculture and designates individuals' roles. The opportunity arises later for me to interview a registered nurse (RN) about this. She tells me that all RNs wear clothing called "scrubs" but style and color have no significance in this hospital; in some hospitals where she has worked color or style of scrubs denotes the specialty department where the RN works. She asks me if I'd noticed that the white coats worn by doctors are of differing lengths. I have not. The nurse tells me that longer coats signify that the physician has had additional education and training (such as a specialist); these coats are knee length. Interns have graduated from medical school but are not yet fully licensed; interns wear hip-length coats. Medical students who have not yet graduated from medical school wear short lab coats. The hospital "natives" recognize these coat-length differences and treat those who wear them accordingly.

After asking my husband a series of detailed questions (birth date, social security number, home address, purpose of the hospital visit) the pre-op person fills out additional forms for his signature. She tells us to note and use the hand sanitizer dispensers that are available at the entrance to each room or area in the hospital. She emphasizes that we should use them both when we enter areas and when we leave. Ah, I say to myself, I've discovered a "rule" of this microculture. While I am waiting for my husband to have his blood taken, I count three hospital employees who enter and leave the waiting room area *without* using hand sanitizer. I ponder if this is an ***ideal vs. real cultural value*** within the hospital or if it is only required of visitors. I will keep watching. I later ask a nurse about this issue. She assures me that there are so many hand sanitizer dispensers in the hospital that staff will use ones other than those in waiting areas. OK, I think to myself, but what about germs encountered while opening a door? If I were an employee of an applied anthropology consulting firm that was hired to investigate this hospital's sanitation practices to prevent the spread of MRSA and other bacterial infections, I would make many more observations and quantify them. Also, I would interview many staff, patients, and visitors about this issue. I have a friend, a registered nurse, who was employed to help another hospital reduce their incidence of such infections. She discovered through hours of observations in the ICU (Intensive Care Unit) that doctors were not as meticulous about hand washing or other protocols as they verbally claimed. Extensive field observations often reveal discrepancies like this one. The hospital's infection rate declined dramatically when *stringent* hand-washing protocols were later initiated. This was a perfect example of cultural ideal vs. real behaviors.

I decide to attempt establishing a bit of rapport with the pre-op nurse who seems quite busy and somewhat stressed. I comment that surely the hospital could provide a larger cubicle for her work. She sighs and says that everyone is currently crowded. I ask if the photos on her bulletin board are her grandchildren, and I note that we have two young grandchildren. Her official mask drops away and she smiles and launches into a brief description of her grandson's recent accomplishments. I ponder that incoming patients might well receive only professional treatment that doesn't feel very personal if they are frightened and don't attempt to establish rapport. Might "professional only" treatment be an element that contributes to new patients experiencing culture shock in this microculture? After some pre-op tests are completed, we are told to return the next day at 6:00 AM.

Culture shock creates anxiety and stress. Culture shock is the term used by anthropologists to describe resultant feelings of helplessness, disorientation, frustration, and even anger that a person encounters after he or she is exposed to an unfamiliar culture, subculture, or microculture. Many small, unfamiliar sights, behaviors, customs, and values together contribute to these feelings. A hospital is one microcultural setting in one's own community where culture shock may be experienced.

I continued my observations of the hospital as a microculture the next day with a focus on the issue of culture shock. I think about ethnographers entering field settings. Many of them write of how they felt and what they noted during their initial experience in "the field." One recurrent theme I've noted reflects my own feelings when doing fieldwork. Initially you feel much like a stranger; you don't understand many aspects of this culture and it makes you disoriented and anxious. People talk to you differently than they do to each other; you are an adult but are being treated in many ways like a child; for example, people may speak very slowly to you. R. Lincoln Keiser who carried out fieldwork with Chicago street gangs noted that he initially couldn't determine when to be afraid, such as one day when a member of another gang entered the neighborhood. Everyone else had slowly moved out of the possible line of gunfire before someone grabbed him and pulled him out of the way. Such incidents underscore one's helplessness, and resulting stress, when in a new culture or microculture.

My husband, when asked, admits to me that he is having "a bit" of culture shock. This is a man who has enjoyed good health all of his life and has had little experience with this microculture. The worst part, he says, is the feeling that he does not have control of the situation. The "natives" are in charge. It makes him anxious. Together we chat and recall both our own fieldwork experiences and those reported by others. Culture shock is usually unexpected and, as such, causes quite a bit of anxiety until you suddenly say: "Wow, I'm experiencing culture shock." Somehow this helps put things in perspective.

When people travel through unfamiliar cultural settings they note things that are "different" from what they are accustomed to. Tourists do this. But tourists often travel with members of their own culture. This creates a comfort zone where differences may be discussed but one need not "deal" with them. They see a culture's important historical sites, museums, and choreographed cultural events as they are shepherded by tour guides. Much is hidden because tourism is an important economic commodity for many countries, and they don't want "customers" to feel uncomfortable with what they see, hear, or even smell! Tourists are just visiting and in a week or two return to the comfort of their own culture. If one experiences an alien culture without the supervision of a "guide," there is a qualitative difference to the experience.

Entering a hospital may have the same effects as being immersed in a foreign culture. The natives know each other, where the yellow line leads (and the red and blue lines), and what will take place during surgery. Hospital natives should keep this perspective in mind as they deal with nonnative "visitors." After all, the goal of hospitals is to improve one's physical health. Anxiety and stress, studies have proved, do not contribute in a positive way to achieving this goal.

Other microcultural experiences that may result in culture shock include attending college as a returning student after years outside of this

40

setting. A 30-something woman in one of my classes shared, as we discussed culture shock during the second week of class, that she felt exactly that way—anxious, disoriented, frustrated, helpless—when she first enrolled at the college after being out of high school for a dozen years. She found that all of this dissipated over time as she became acquainted with the student culture on campus. She said that she was relieved to know that her reaction wasn't uncommon and actually had a term to describe it. Starting a new job, particularly if it is in a new community and outside of your area of expertise, may have the same effect: You end up with a headache each day, don't understand much of the office culture, feel anxious, and wonder if it was a mistake to have taken the job. A short orientation meeting offered by colleges or corporations may give a person some insights, but immersion in that new microculture often leads to some culture shock.

Most seasoned anthropologists will admit to experiencing culture shock during their initial periods of fieldwork, despite all of the preparation and background-checking they do before setting out. A former linguistics specialist professor of mine told how he was sure that he would not fall victim to culture shock because he had prepared thoroughly, knew the language, and considered himself to be "tough." He reported that he was so overwhelmed with feelings of helplessness and disorientation after several weeks on his own, in a busy Indian community near New Delhi, that he actually cried, something he had not done even as a child. He had read everything he could about India. He talked to other anthropologists who had been studying in communities adjacent to where his work would take place. But he said it wasn't "real" until he was there seeing people with various skin diseases such as leprosy up close, being jostled by crowds of humanity, smelling unfamiliar scents, and walking past gutters flowing with human waste.

Returning to one's own culture after being immersed in another culture often results in culture shock, too. Many say it can be more of a problem than what they experienced living in a foreign culture. I recall how I hated going to supermarkets on my return to the states after living in a

41

small village in Spain. My return culture shock was caused by too many choices here—breakfast in the village had consisted of choosing between the two cereal box offerings available at the small one-room village store, and evening dinner came from what local fishermen caught that morning. Back in the states the crowded stores were filled with strangers who generally avoided eye contact and never greeted me. In Spain everyone greeted everyone and often stopped to chat.

Men and women returning from combat zones often experience not only culture shock but the now well-publicized post-traumatic stress syndrome. Missionaries, diplomats, and Peace Corps workers frequently exhibit this return culture shock, too, depending on how long they were away and how immersed they became in the foreign culture.

Use the anthropological perspective every day. Treating a hospital or other microculture as "foreign culture" and applying anthropological methods and insights, such as culture shock, can be interesting and very rewarding. Oh yes, my husband's surgery was successful.

Challenge: Reflect on a time when you visited a microculture with which you were not familiar. In retrospect did you experience any culture shock?

***

Thinking It Through
- Describe the basic fieldwork process of ethnography and participant observation.
- Identify a microculture and examples of ideal and actual practices found within it.
- Explore the value of establishing rapport in everyday situations.
- Describe culture shock and its symptoms.

Anthropological Terms
culture	ideal vs. real cultural value
culture shock	microculture
establishing rapport	participant observation

Thinking Practically

- Interview a person who experienced a job change recently (particularly if the new job is vastly different from the previous one). Explain culture shock to the person and ask if he or she experienced any of its symptoms. Share that anthropologists identify this as a common occurrence when one is in an unfamiliar culture, subculture, or microculture.
- Describe culture shock to a returning or new student at your college. Ask the person to reflect on her or his first few weeks back in school. Can the person identify any symptoms of culture shock?

6 ~ The Purple House

Culture's influence in everyday life is demonstrated in what we think about color and how our values and attitudes are learned (through enculturation) and evolve through diffusion and cyclical change. Additional perspective is gained through the comparative linguistic analysis of color lexicons.

Purple!!! The house is painted purple. What were they thinking? I say to myself as I gaze along the block of stucco-finished, middle-class, single-story houses. I note that other homes on both sides of the street present an array of tasteful, muted earthy hues (hues are colors dependent on their dominant wavelengths, independent of intensity) from cream and tan to light, pale grays, greens, and light golden shades. I actually think "tasteful," and then I immediately chuckle to myself and check my ***ethnocentrism***. What is tasteful and correct when it comes to color of houses and other artifacts and features is encultured. *Enculturation*, the process of learning one's culture while growing up in it, is powerful. Even trained anthropologists are not immune to reactions based on our cultural upbringing.

Have you noticed apartments, condominiums, and town houses adjacent to freeways in North America? Miles of white and pale shades of earth colors dot the landscape. This is also apparent in most single-family and multiple-family one- and two-story homes in both suburbs and cities. Besides cultural tradition, local homeowner association rules often require approval before any exterior painting is done. Bright, bold exteriors in primary colors are typically forbidden and the above-mentioned hues dictated as appropriate. Occasionally vividly colored houses are encountered in areas without homeowners' associations. These may be occupied by a first-generation immigrant enculturated with different ideas and attitudes about color. I suspect this is the case with the purple house that is located in the culturally diverse Central Valley of California.

House color trends change over time. In the city of San Francisco, California, the vogue in recent decades has been for vintage 1890s' Victorian homes to be painted with colors other than the uniform white popular in the mid-twentieth century. What has been labeled the Colorist Movement began here in the 1960s when hippies started to paint a few old Victorians in bright psychedelic colors. Despite some grumbling by other citizens who called these houses "weird" and in "shocking bad taste," the color trend increased and ultimately diffused across America and to Europe. By the late 1970s and into the twenty-first century increasing numbers of San Francisco Victorians were painted with diverse colors. The Alamo Square area of the city is the location of homes known as the Painted Ladies. To earn this title houses have to show three or more contrasting colors and often exhibit nine to 15 colors, plus they might be gilded with gold leaf. One or two focal colors are used—lavender, purple, burgundy, blue, blue-gray, dark teal, gray green, dusty rose, pale pink— with numerous shadings and combinations of each color; white and black are sometimes used as well on the gingerbread trims. Houses thus painted are described as tasteful, artistic, and not excessively showy.

The painting of Victorians became quite competitive. Such painting is expensive because the paint is applied by hand. I've often thought this an example of what I term present-day *potlatching* (see "Potlatch?" essay, this volume)—where financially able individuals gain attention and social status by displaying their wealth, in this case owning an admired and talked about house. Recently the style in demand (according to a long-time house painter in the city with whom I spoke) is to tone down exterior colors and use only three. He told me the young wealthy "techies" that are now buying Victorians are demanding hip nearly monochromatic looks in house paint (both inside and out). Is this evidence of the onset of another cyclical style change in American culture?

Anthropologists have identified the mechanisms of stylistic changes in cultures historically and across the globe. We use the term *diffusion* to refer to the spread of ideas or artifacts between cultures. Diffusion can happen when individuals travel short or long distances—walking, on horseback, or riding camels—and return home bringing an idea from the culture they visited. Archaeologists and historians have documented this process happening over at least 10,000 years of human history. Today, travel or something seen on Facebook or YouTube may be the means of contact with other ideas that diffuse and are integrated into one's own culture. *Cyclical change* is culture change observed and documented to fluctuate in cycles over a period of years. Both diffusion and cyclical change are readily documented in where and how color was and is used. And, of course economics plays a role in both.

Color is big business. Global media encourage and teach (or some critics think they dictate) how we should think about color and what we should do about and with it—and people comply. No one wants to be "outdated." Take, for example, the campaigns by paint manufacturers and the home-decorating industry to influence our use of color. The colors touted in these campaigns are cyclical. A few years ago advertisements showed home paint colors in shades of "muted custard," "roasted corn," and "marshmallow cream." More recently gray hues dominate with names like "legendary gray," "gray frost," "metropolis," and "elephant's breath."

As I ponder how ideas about color "correctness" are learned and change, my thoughts expand. I run through mental images of the exterior house colors I've seen in my travels and the ones shown on nightly televised international news reports. I lived for a time in a Spanish village that dated to the sixteenth century. All structures, if painted, were whitewashed, but most houses and apartments were unpainted blocks of quarried local stone of a soft golden hue. Newer structures were often built of cement blocks painted white. Window shutters were painted soft greens or rust. I felt comfortable in this surrounding as is usually the case when one encounters another culture with a custom similar to one's own. In my experiences in several remote areas on Polynesian islands 45 years ago, many homes and businesses were constructed of imported cement blocks. These were whitewashed or they retained the original light gray color of cement. Televised news of global events today sometimes gives glimpses of housing in different parts of the world, and much of it is of unpainted native stone or bricks.

International tourism in recent years is responsible for encouraging the diffusion of colorfully painted neighborhoods, particularly commercial buildings. Brightly colored houses and shops make interesting photos for postcards and photo postings on Facebook. Marketing advertisements and brochures often focus on areas where shop owners have paid attention to the appeal and drawing power of paint color. Portobello Road in London, England, is a favorite of many travelers who enjoy seeing the brightly colored store- and housefronts; the nearby Notting Hill district, with houses of reds, blues, and other lively hues, is also a popular tourist stop. I recall my first visit to these areas when the storefronts and homes were monochromatic. It was an interesting place to shop then with its many antique stores, but now it has the added enticement of lively visages. This trend in tourist locations is apparent around the world. If you Google a prompt like "colorful world cities" or "colorful storefronts and housing" you'll get a plethora of hits such as downtown Ennis in Galway, Ireland; Burano Island, Italy; Reykjavik, Iceland; Cinque Terra, Italy; Bo-Kaap, Cape Town, South Africa. The economies of many world countries depend upon tourist dollars.

I reflect on why I reacted the way I did to the purple house. We feel comfort in the familiar. The familiar once meant one's own family, community, or *microculture*. The culture we are born into stamps upon us many such fundamental ideas. Until the age of seven I lived in a Southern California neighborhood of 1930s' vintage-era houses with clapboard siding exteriors. All were painted varied shades of white. When my family moved to the suburbs and a newly built tract house all homes had stucco exteriors of pale washed-out hues of tan, white, gray, green, or gold. These colors were so minimal as to be barely noticeable. I absorbed the cultural idea that houses should not be bright colors. When we leave our home area and travel we often note colorful storefronts and colorful homes and consider them bold, cute, or fun because they are different from what most of us experience daily. Yet we would not feel comfortable painting our house a vivid color. Travel is an adventure, and travel experiences usually stay with us as that; we rarely bring them home except as happy memories. Our enculturation wins out.

In the early days of the discipline, anthropological linguists collected information on aspects of language content and structure. One focal point was on color vocabularies (*lexicons*). Some anthropological linguists wondered if actual physiological differences existed between cultural groups in how the eye and brain perceive and interpret colors; the hypothesis they developed considered evolutionary reasons for these differences. We now know from many scientific studies that all human eyes are physiologically the same with regard to types of cells—the rods and cones of the eye—and their detection of variation in light intensity and wavelength, in other words how we detect color. Other linguists hypothesized that lexicon differences were due to cultural learning about what to differentiate in the environment. Comparative data demonstrate that in some languages color vocabularies have only a few words for colors. Speakers of those languages can differentiate colors but in daily use do not do so; closely related hues are simply lumped under a single-color word. For example, the Dugum Dani of the Papua New Guinea highlands use two words for color. Rosch, who studied their language extensively, reports these two basic color words as *mola* and *mili*. Mola describes warm colors such as reds, orange, yellow, reddish purple, light browns plus white. Mili covers all cooler colors such as greens and blues plus dark browns and black (Foley 2000: 154). Note: There is some debate regarding languages with only two or three terms for color and whether brightness of the hue plays a role in which term is selected by an individual speaker. Other languages contain an extensive number of words for color; the number of basic language color terminologies as reported by Berlin and Kay (1969) based on their study of data from 98 languages ranges from a minimum of two to a maximum of 11 (Berlin and Kay 1969; Bonvillain 2014; Kay 2000). Consider how people who speak different languages describe the colors of a rainbow. English speakers usually name seven colors when viewing a rainbow—red, orange, yellow, green, blue, indigo (the color between blue and violet often called purple), and violet. Shona speakers of West Africa use only three words for colors. They group orange, red, and purple under one word. Another word is used to describe blue and green-blue, while another single word is used to describe yellow and yellow-green. Quite a few other languages similarly group several colors under a single word. Comparative linguistic research establishes that more lexicons only give people more detail in what is important in their culture, they don't dictate a different reality.

Does our choice of a house color connect to the symbolism of colors as we are enculturated to think of them—this color is warm, that cold, this one means danger, that one means safety? Anthropology's comparative approach reveals both differences and similarities in what a color symbolizes in cultures globally. Red signifies power in North America while in Russia it symbolizes revolution. White symbolizes purity in North America and is associated with death and mourning in China and also symbolizes mourning in Brazil and Thailand. Purple is associated with royalty, faith, and honor in much of Europe and North America and happiness to the Navaho.

Fast, worldwide internet connections to social and other media increase the potential for the diffusion of symbolic colors to other cultures. An animated film, *Inside Out* (June 2015), underscores this. It illustrates how color may be used to symbolize emotion and mood as conceived by the filmmakers. Colors were assigned to the film's animated cartoon characters; these colors intensified when the characters expressed various emotions such as anger (red), joy (yellow), fear (purple), disgust (green), and sadness (blue). We took my young grandchildren to this movie. Following the film my husband and I discussed what influence the color choices (made by the writers and producers) for each mood or emotion might have on the enculturation of children globally.

Color in its various contexts is a good place to begin thinking of all of the ways our cultures impact us in how we think, what we believe, and what we do every day. In the past, enculturation came primarily through contact with family and community. Today advertisements, commercials, and social media posts have become part of a larger circle of influence in the enculturation process for each of us. What's in your head when you see a purple house? And what culture or microculture put it there?

Challenge: What color is your car? Why did you or your family choose this color?

Thinking It Through
- Discuss how cultural misunderstandings over the use of colors could impact business dealings internationally.
- If your home, or a room in it, has been repainted recently, describe the process by which a color was selected. Which individuals were most influential in the final color choice?

Anthropological Terms
cyclical change	lexicon
diffusion	microculture
enculturation	potlatch
ethnocentrism	

Thinking Practically
- Discuss how you think your neighbors would react to your painting your house purple with orange trim? How would *you* react to your neighbor painting her house in those colors?
- Ask several elders what car colors were popular when they were in high school. Have these colors returned to popularity?

7 ~ Grass and Class

North Americans like to think of themselves as part of an egalitarian, classless society grounded in our nation's Declaration of Independence. This essay illustrates how a social class–like stratification creeps into our everyday experiences.

It is a sunny October morning. No clouds. Blue sky. I'm on my morning walk. I turn the corner and pause in front of a home that has a front yard consisting of brown grass, exposed dirt, and a cemetery tableau. It is filled with tombstones and a few scattered human bones. I identify a femur, a humerus, and a parietal (part of the skull) plus a half unearthed complete human skeleton lying on its back. There is also a complete skeleton lying on the home's roof. It has one hand grasping the hand of a second skeleton that is dangling over the side of the roof. This elaborate Halloween tableau is one of many I've encountered recently when rambling around this San Francisco Bay Area suburb I call home. I smile as I glance across the street where a home's lawn shows large brown areas. Its porch is filled with pumpkins, and a broom riding witch is impaled on the trunk of the front yard tree, her arms hugging the bark, her nose imbedded, and her broom handle poking through to the opposite side of the tree trunk. I feel an odd premonition of something as I scan up and down the block of houses. It is not Halloween spirits that evokes this uneasy, nagging feeling. I look around again. I'm missing something. What is it?

Abruptly it springs into focus. It is grass! No, not that kind; although anthropologists do and have studied mind-altering drugs and how people use them in various *cultures*. Lawn grass. Dying lawns. We are in the fifth year of a serious drought. I begin to retrace this morning's steps. I'm observing an everyday example of *social class* in America! I often slip on my anthropological lenses; these let me see the familiar as a stranger— someone of a different world culture or perhaps an extraterrestrial visitor—might see it. My perspective is a result of my background in anthropology's extensive use of the *comparative method*.

Lawn grass is not part of the coverage of social class typically analyzed in media essays such as in *The New York Times* or *The Atlantic*. Nor is it usually included when social class or inequity is discussed on internet blogs, National Public Radio panels, or in college classrooms. Those presentations typically focus on overarching issues of employment, education, income, and demographics as they reflect social class. Grass in home landscapes offers a small everyday visual example of the phenomenon of social class. I'll return to this momentarily.

First some background. The definition, analysis, and theory of social class is messy and complicated. Nineteenth-century theorists Karl Marx and Max Weber are credited with beginning the discussion about and definitions of social class; theoretical discourse today builds on their foundation. Anthropologist Roger Keesing noted 40 years ago: "Social theorists have struggled for three centuries to decide what classes are, and they still do not agree" (Keesing 1976: 340). Today, we can make the same statement. Keesing went on to discuss stratification within societies and offered his definition of social class as: "A division of society, defined in terms of its relationship to the means of production, within a system of such classes, hierarchically ordered, and marked by a consciousness of their collective identity and interests" (ibid. 1976: 567). There are many nuances to the issue and its treatment today in academia. To keep things simple for purposes of this essay I'll use the definition I've given in my text, *Introducing Cultural Anthropology 5/e*. A class is "a group of people who have a similar relationship to wealth, power, and prestige" (Lenkeit 2012: 230).

With daily reports and media coverage of social unrest in some part of the world, I believe that most of us have gained a general understanding of class differences and that these differences are indeed bound by the interplay of wealth, power, and prestige. We know that a particular social class is a group of people who *are aware* of belonging to this group based on their economic standing (wealth) and interests (typically political). This group knows the economic and social standing and interests of other groups. Social classes are labeled in generally accepted social usage as: the poor, lower (or working or blue-collar) class, middle class, and upper class (the elite). Some theorists divide the middle class into three subclasses—lower-middle, middle, and upper-middle.

Anthropologists were relatively late to emphasize an analysis of social class. This was because the discipline focused in its early years (the mid-nineteenth century) on ethnographic descriptions of aboriginal populations. Comparative studies of these ethnographies resulted in grouping societies based on their economic systems—*foragers* (also called hunting and gathering societies or *bands*) and early *horticultural* and *pastoral societies* known as *tribes*. Bands and tribes did not have stratified layers. Rather they were characterized by their *egalitarian* natures. Members of these societies had fairly equal economic stature, and status was achieved not by displaying material wealth but rather by exhibiting outstanding individual skills—best tracker, hunter, curer, or midwife, for example. Individuals had equal access to these roles. Men's and woman's roles were the only distinction in the division of labor.

It is in societies that emerged later in human history, those termed *chiefdom* and *state* societies, that *stratification* is found, resulting in the "class" concept. Both chiefdoms and states are characterized by economic specialization. Chiefdoms have economic specialization and a centralized office of chief who is responsible for an economic redistributive system within the society. Chiefs have status and economic resources, wealth, and power the rest of the population doesn't have. States exhibit much variety—e.g., democratic states, parliamentary states, authoritarian states.

They are legally constituted and complex with stratification, specialization at every level, and wealth is not equally distributed.

Lumping societies into such "types" is an analytical approach that has been challenged by scholars both within and outside the discipline. Yet, when doing meta-analysis of worldwide ethnographic descriptions, fundamental groupings emerge. I acknowledge the incredible complexity and variability of human culture and societies but believe that utilizing basic groupings such as those based on economic systems has merit for purposes of comparison and further analysis. Today many anthropologists are engaged in the analysis of social stratification and class inequities within their own countries and around the world.

Back to my Halloween wanderings and observations of social class within the context of the drought that is gripping California. I determined to do a quick observational study. As I walked, I tabulated that four out of five front-yard landscapes in a one-square-mile area showed the effects of reduced watering—dry, brown lawns, browning shrubs, and an occasional dead tree. Homes in this section currently cost between $450,000 and $800,000 and are about 1,400–2,000 square feet in size (outrageously expensive compared to most of the country!). Locally, they are considered middle class and upper-middle class.

As I progressed in my ramble, I entered an area considered "upscale" (i.e., upper class). Here homes cost 40–50% more and are larger, between 2,500 to 5,000 square feet. In a square-mile section here, I counted only three lawns showing signs of water restriction, and these were homes that had xeriscapes with native plantings. All other homes had well-manicured, lush green lawns and shrubs.

Much of California's geography is technically classified a desert. Water for domestic and agricultural use is dependent on the importation of water and the pumping of ground water. A primary source in the southern part of the state is the Colorado River. This is supplemented by a series of dams, reservoirs, and canals that hold and move water flowing out of the Sierra Nevada mountain range in the northern part of the state. The central and northern parts of the state are also dependent on the

Sierra Nevada snowpack waters and well water. This is a complex issue with much history and politics behind it.

Historically California droughts range up to 10 years, but everyone is hoping the current one will not last so long. The Sierra Nevada snowpack has been below normal for two years in a row, and this year is not promising to alter that. In California's large central valley many rural household wells have already gone dry and more are added to that list each week. Well-digging companies have waiting lists for customers who want to dig deeper wells. One of my friends is on such a list and is very frustrated. The cost of household water is rising as city utility districts struggle to provide safe potable water. Predictions of much higher water utility costs appear weekly in local papers as part of efforts to encourage serious reduction of water usage. The drought has also forced a significant reduction in productive crop land.

California and Bay Area city governments have imposed varying degrees of water conservation rules to get us through this drought. California Governor Jerry Brown issued an executive order in April 2015 mandating a 25 percent reduction in water use and my local city council in May approved an emergency ordinance requiring a 30 percent reduction in domestic water use. Nightly news reports draw attention to ways citizens can save water—reduce lawn watering, replace lawns with drought tolerant plants, don't leave water running during teeth brushing, take shorter showers, keep buckets in the shower and kitchen sink to collect water and then use it on landscape plants. Should the drought continue many experts predict dire outcomes.

Green grass lawns, weedless and groomed (mowing and edging), offer an example and illustrate the "learned" and "shared" aspects of culture in the lives of individuals living in most regions of North America. We grow up surrounded by such lawns; we watch our parents mow and care for them; often we inherit the job of mowing them when we reach our teens, especially boys—gender-based family-assigned chores are another aspect of our culture. We see cartoons in our newspapers about Dad mowing the lawn or complaining about the task (e.g., *Zits* and *Baby*

Blues). We see ads for garden products on television and view green lawns portrayed in commercials, on television shows, and in movies. We learn to value lawns, and we learn to view green, manicured lawns as a required standard within middle- and upper-class neighborhoods.

We don't eat the grass or feed it to our animals. Where did this obsession originate? Consider how an individual from the highlands of New Guinea, the Siberian Steppes, a village in West Africa, a Polynesian island village, or a Middle Eastern country might react when seeing suburban neighborhoods of North America for the first time. Many contemporary cultures manage just fine without green lawns; other social issues are the focus of class status in those societies.

Most early immigrants to North America came from European countries. There the upper-class "gentry" lived on huge estates surrounded by lush lawns and elaborate gardens—think of the landscape of the 5,000 acre estate Highclere Castle portrayed in the popular television drama *Downton Abbey*. This idea of green grass lawns was exported to other world regions during the colonial period. Today, these estates are often included on European tour itineraries showing how the wealthy lived in past times. Lawns were one of the outward symbols of "making it." As our forebears transitioned from the hard work of merely putting food on the table they began using extra money and time to create lawns and gardens of their own. In much of North America summer rains took care of watering such landscapes. In desert regions the importation of water and pumping ground water made green laws possible. A green grass lawn in desert climates goes against scientific reason. But this cultural heritage keeps those of us who live in California and in other arid states planting and maintaining lawns—until we are hit by a prolonged drought. Brown grass versus green grass is a current topic of conversation when people gather and chat. In letters to the editor or on social media individuals are complaining that they are doing their part to reduce water usage during the drought but the wealthy (upper class) ignore the issue and continue to use all of the water necessary to keep their landscape grass lush and green.

The United States Geological Survey (2016) indicates that 80–100 gallons is the range of water usage for most individuals per day. Most California utilities charge a penalty if water usage exceeds a designated amount per household per month. Investigative reporting in this, the fifth year of the current drought, has exposed wealthy housing enclaves as "water hogs" and "guzzlers" that do not do their part to conserve. Here are some examples of the available data from 2014 through 2015: in Rancho Santa Fe, San Diego County (listed as one of the nation's richest zip codes), use was 584.4 gallons of water per person per day; Beverly Hills residents used 285.6 gallons, while Los Angeles residents used only 92.8. In Northern California, the Silicon Valley enclave of Hillsborough consumed 290 gallons per day, while the nearby city of Menlo Park recorded a mere 55.8 gallons per day (Woody 2014).

The East Bay Municipal Utility District (EBMUD) in the San Francisco Bay Area reported that average EBMUD household customer uses less than 250 gallons per day. In the small community of Saddleback, 28 households (of 53 in the community) used more than 1,000 gallons per day and they paid high fines for it. One resident consumed 5,996 gallons a day; another used 12,580 gallons (Brekke 2015).

Water is a commodity. The majority of upper-class home owners, based on viewing their landscaped homes and water consumption statistics, appear to have the attitude that they don't need to conserve water. They just pay for it. In other words, this group or class (that could also be called a microculture) has a similar relationship to wealth—they own expensive homes and have the economic resources to pay water bills of thousands of dollars per month plus fines for excess usage, so they do. Additionally, people in this group have the power to influence utility districts and regulatory agencies to overlook their lack of participating, with the rest of the citizenry, in water conservation. Growing grass (lawn grass!) and water conservation issues illustrate one everyday visible aspect of class in American society.

Challenge: Ask a friend what he or she understands "social class" to mean. Gently discourage your friend from whipping out a cell phone and going to Wikipedia. (You are interested in what your friend thinks of the term.) Ask your friend to provide an example experienced firsthand.

Thinking It Through
- Discuss how the concept of culture is illustrated in the case of home owners desiring that their homes be surrounded by green grass.
- Describe the three aspects of social class emphasized by the author. Cite an example of how middle class differs from upper class as you understand these social classes.
- Explain how water usage can be used to illustrate class differences in North American society during a drought.

Anthropological Terms

band	horticultural society
chiefdom	pastoral society
comparative method	social class
culture	state
egalitarian	stratification
forager	tribe

Thinking Practically
- Describe how television automotive commercials can be interpreted as a vehicle (couldn't resist this!) that is reinforcing social classes in North American society.
- Identify two features of members of your community who are identified by members of your community as upper class.

8 ~ High Heels and Bound Feet

This essay explores, with an emphasis on footwear, how culture and the enculturation process have a profound effect on individual behaviors associated with body image.

Overheard yesterday, a Monday, in a theater restroom: "My back is killing me today and my feet hurt. This always happens when I wear my three-inch heels to church." This comment sent me yet again to pondering the influence of human ***culture*** on individual behaviors and the ***ethnocentrism*** that is its companion.

Glossy magazine advertisements feature them; red-carpet cameras focus on them; Lady Gaga struts in them; career women, teens, 20-somethings and beyond lust after three- and four-inch high-heeled shoes and equally high platform shoes. How and why are these popular yet again? Are we, said a voice in my head, rational, free-thinking beings or only another generation of sheep baaing endlessly as we follow the herd while telling ourselves that we are individuals? My anthropology voice reminded me to use my anthropological lens to consider this issue.

We humans learn by observation, imitation, trial and error, and through language. Little girls see their mothers, and other women, wearing high-heeled shoes. A shopping trip with mom may include children observing mom pause to view displays of these shoes. When mom dresses up she puts on "dress-up" shoes that are typically high heels. As children grow, they are bombarded by images of pop, movie, and entertainment stars, and models wearing high heels that are often brightly colored and adorned with rhinestones. The popular television show *Dancing with the Stars* shows the women stars dancing to the rhythm of demanding and athletically challenging music while wearing spiked high heels. Business-women and female politicians are seen wearing high heels, too, although usually plain-colored ones. Little girls playing dress-up clomp around in mom's high-heeled shoes. Barbie and other dolls come with wardrobes that include high-heeled shoes. Little boys take note of all of this.

The message is everywhere—legs look good and look "sexy" in high-heeled shoes, not in flats. A foot encased in a high-heeled shoe, with the wearer's heel as much as three inches higher than the ball of the foot and toes, appears smaller than it really is. The shape of the leg when wearing high heels gives the overall illusion of being long and slim. Also, the shape of the buttocks is emphasized when standing on the ball of the foot. These features and our attitudes toward them are part of our culture. These learned, shared, socially transmitted values and behaviors mold us and the choices we make.

Other cultures mold and continue to shape the behaviors and values of their children, too. Many have heard of the historical tradition of foot binding in China. We are usually quite ethnocentric in our views about it and say what a terrible, brutal custom it was. Such views rarely note that the binding of the feet of young girls in China was at one time considered a rite of passage for daughters of the higher classes. The process gave girls tiny narrow dainty feet—an ideal foot length called the Golden Lotus was a mere 7 cm (3″)—making them more beautiful and desirable. Bound feet were considered sexually stimulating to men. The foot binding began in childhood and consisted of folding the toes under and binding them ever tighter to the sole of the foot. The toes broke. Bandages were tight-ened until the foot protruded almost completely straight from the leg, and the arch was forcibly broken in the process. The resulting deformity was a shorter, arched, and pointed foot (the great toe was not bent). Of course flesh often died and infections were common. Bound feet changed the way girls walked, making them take short steps and sway from side to side as they learned to balance on the misshapen (and painful) feet shod in special slippers. This walk was a mark of refinement; it was considered sexy. The custom has been prohibited in China since 1911. Recent writings, both memoirs and fiction, include descriptions of the custom and reasons why it was accepted and desired. Can a contemporary woman read of this outdated custom without a shocked ethnocentric reaction and an inner voice cheering her luck in being born in enlightened times?

Body modification customs are known from both the recent past and contemporary societies. The Victorian custom of corsets cinching women's waists to make them smaller and create perfect, sexually attractive figures is one example from history. Many past cultures around the globe had traditions of altering the shape of the skull through binding infants' skulls, as noted in writings from as early as 400 BC. Perhaps the best-known examples are of the prehistoric Inca and Maya traditions of flattening the forehead by binding infants' skulls so that the forehead sloped back from the top of the nose.

Placing neck rings around women's necks is a traditional custom still practiced today in some contemporary Southeast Asian cultures such as the Meo of Thailand. The custom involves placing brass coils or rings around the necks of young girls adding more over time until the neck appears quite elongated. In fact, the neck does not lengthen, rather the collarbone and shoulders are forced down and are deformed. Not all women of these cultures wear the rings today. However, tourism is partly (some say wholly) responsible for the continuation of the custom because tourists, with their money, seek to photograph women with the rings.

Consider the customs discussed above, view them through the lens of anthropology, and then turn the lens on your own world.

When I lived in northern Spain doing fieldwork some of the locals still wore *albarcas*. These are clog-like shoes carved out of wood that are elevated by three 1¼- to 1½-inch-high and 1¼-inch-wide wooden pegs. Two of the pegs are under the ball of the foot section of the shoe (one is near each outer edge) and one peg is under the center of the heel. Informants told me that generations of people wore these *albarcas* outside on wet cobbled streets and while working in muddy gardens and fields; they were easy to slip out of and replace with slippers when entering one's home. These elevated shoes had a purpose. They did not alter the shape of the foot, or leg, and did not have ill effects on muscles or tendons. I have a pair of these and find them quite stable, owing to the tripod-like placement of the pegs. There are other historical and worldwide examples of elevated shoes that provide similar functions. Fashion high heels do not fulfill any purpose other than style.

Today, many influential sources of information teach us to be dissatisfied with our bodies. My local paper regularly carries advertisements for various forms of cosmetic surgery. Besides the most popular alterations to noses, faces, and breasts, one can create a "better self" (read "conform to societal ideals") by enhancing or sculpting one's butt, calves, and even pursuing the latest rage of remodeling one's private parts (to appear younger and be more taut). How does one resist these artificially created ideas of beauty when such messages, both direct and subliminal, are everywhere?

I remember the cultural and peer pressures to conform from my own youth. In high school I got my first "heels." I can clearly see them if I close my eyes—white with a swirly, thin line of leather across the toe box, edged in gold, and sporting 3½-inch heels. All of my girlfriends joined in this important event. This made us "grown-up" and gave us "sex appeal." We all wore them to events in college, even on dates to football games. Uncomfortable, yes, but we wouldn't think of not wearing them on dates.

Then came the women's movement of the late 1960s and the 1970s and 1980s. Burn your bras and girdles and throw away those uncomfortable (and scientifically proven to cause numerous foot, back, and knee problems) high heels. Yet, most of us still wore them as we graduated and took our first jobs. They were considered part of proper "business attire" for women in banks, offices, and corporate America as well as proper "social attire" at church, weddings, funerals, and artistic events. I recall standing for hours in them as I lectured about culture and human biological evolution to my college students. My feet hurt and my back was beginning to suffer. But subtle voices including that of my husband

("Your legs look sexy in those new shoes.") and parents ("You look so professional in that outfit.") continued to reinforce this behavior.

You may ask how I could talk of issues of culture and customs of other cultures, including ones that were known by Western science to be, if not down right unhealthy, at least detrimental to women's health, and continue to wear these shoes. My anthropological voice whispered "*cultural tradition*" while my scientific background growled "ridiculous, unhealthy." Well, one day my aching feet and science won; I faced the issue and stopped wearing high heels. Somewhat to my surprise other professors, though not the support staff or administrative workers, began to do the same. Was my revolt to be the little grain of sand that would initiate an avalanche? Apparently not.

While there was a small trend to lower heels and flat shoes in the late 1970s and 1980s, a new generation is now embracing high heels. New forms of media and advertisements help fuel fashion trends and cultural values even as podiatrists and scientists present evidence that such shoes cause many medical problems—bunions, shortened calf muscles, lower-back pain, knee problems (including contributing to osteoarthritis of the knee), and leg and foot pain. Additionally, the havoc rendered from twisted ankles, falls, and broken bones resulting from balancing on these shoes is well documented. In one recent article a woman doctor describes all of the reasons that one should shun high heels. Yet, in her conclusion she admits that she still wears them when she dresses up. In another article a male podiatrist, after listing all of the reasons not to wear heels, remarked that legs look better in high heels. What you wear, your attitudes about your body, and how you treat it are learned, shared, and socially transmitted. How will future generations view our love affair with high heels?

Update 2019: Yesterday I leafed through several magazines while getting my hair trimmed by my high heel, platform shoe–clad stylist. Pages of advertisements and celebrity photos showed women wearing Christian Louboutin, Manolo Blahnik, and Jimmy Chow designer shoes, so stiletto and other high heels are still popular. While I thought about this, I also

65

contemplated a recent article I had read regarding women continuing to seek orthopedic procedures to alter their feet to fit the shoes they love, such as the shortening of toes and other surgery (often referred to as a "Cinderella" procedure or "stiletto surgery" or "Loub Job") (Breslow 2018). I muse on whether our descendants will look back a hundred years from now and compare what women are willing to bear for fashion with how we view foot binding traditions of centuries ago.

Challenge: Culture is powerful. I challenge you to consider how your culture has shaped your behaviors and attitudes about cosmetics, tattoos, and high heels.

Thinking It Through
- Examine how culture influences behavior.
- Compare cross-cultural examples of body modification and how such customs can persist.

Anthropological Terms
    cultural tradition
    culture
    ethnocentrism

Thinking Practically
- Consider your own enculturation. Identify and rank two specific learning experiences that formed your attitude toward cosmetic plastic surgery.
- Compare the practice of bound feet with the wearing of high-heeled shoes.

9 ~ White Teeth

*When her dental hygienist called teeth whitening the new
anorexia, the author reviewed the issue. She contemplates the
ability of individuals and the media to influence cultural
attitudes and examines the process of culture change.*

What do you think of teeth whitening? I queried my dental hygienist.
She didn't even need to think about it but fired back a reply: "It is the
new anorexia." She went on to tell of young patients begging the dentist
to whiten their teeth. They often carried magazines with glossy photos of
models, musicians, moguls, and movie stars to show their dentist how
they wanted their smile to look. My dentist declines to whiten the teeth
of persons under 18 years of age. We are told that whitening agents are
safe and do no harm, but they have been widely used for only a little over
a decade. Long-term effects are, in fact, unknown.

From my vantage point as a cultural anthropologist, I watched the
unfolding of the white-teeth craze with heightened appreciation for the
impact of culture. The fad, born in the corporate culture of profit-seek-
ing dental-product manufacturers, shows little inclination to abate. I
recall one of my anthropology professor's analysis of the failure in the
1980s of a major toothpaste brand (that promised white teeth) to succeed
in an Asian country because everyone displayed discolored teeth. They
chewed betel nuts. People with monetary resources could afford a steady
supply of betel nuts; discolored teeth thus became an outward sign that

one was a person of means and high status. The idea of using toothpaste to whiten one's teeth brought instant rejection, and the whitening toothpaste failed miserably.

The betel nut is the seed of the areca palm. Areca nut (betel nut) chewing has been popular for centuries in Southeast Asia and the South Pacific where the areca palm grows. The betel nut has a stimulant effect on those that ingest it, and some report feeling euphoric. Slices of the nut are wrapped in leaves, mixed with powdered lime (the mineral, not the fruit), and sometimes seasonings are added; they are often artistically presented in slices on a plate similar to how hors d'oeuvres are presented. The leaf-wrapped packet is typically placed between the teeth and cheek where it is pressed, chewed, and sucked on as the ingredients mix with saliva. Saliva mixes with chemicals in the nut, creating a red color. Gums, lips, and tooth enamel become stained red—longtime users' teeth are stained black. Much of the saliva produced is spit out. In addition to everyday use, betel nuts are included in many customs associated with hospitality, marriage, and religion. In other words chewing betel nuts is part of the *fabric of cultures* in this region. The custom is learned and shared and transmitted socially from generation to generation. People are accustomed to discolored smiles.

Persons of Western cultures often react ethnocentrically when seeing a red-stained smile caused by the regular ingestion of betel nuts—thinking how ugly it looks, or at least how curious it looks, and wondering why would one want to have red-stained teeth. And, of course, all the while the visitor is exhibiting white and whiter teeth based on current norms within his or her culture.

I recall my fascination as a small child with my grandpa's very white, very perfect teeth. He'd catch me staring and smile more broadly, then push out the lower plate. I'd scream and run away. As I grew older I'd merely giggle. We did quite a bit of bonding because of those false teeth, and I recall the *ick* factor when he visited and I'd see the teeth sitting in a glass of water in the bathroom. To me the new white teeth look like my grandfather's false teeth. Plastic. Not real. Clearly dentistry these days can make natural-looking replacement teeth, and there are likely people you know that have one or more "false teeth" in the form of bridges, veneers, or implants, and you can't even tell that they aren't natural teeth. But grandpa's teeth looked fake, all colored bright white.

Real tooth enamel is not a blinding white, white. Children's teeth (being new!) are whiter than an adults' teeth. Enamel darkens due to foods and drinks that stain, changes in the mineral structure of the teeth, and certain medications. Plus there is genetic variation in enamel color. Why does our culture not celebrate the variation, or at least ignore it?

The subtle learning by observation during childhood (part of the *enculturation* process) has a profound effect on everyone in every *culture*. Children hear adults talking about white teeth. They see magazine, television, and internet advertisements promoting white teeth. Consequently, there is little wonder that Western folk, and now increasingly people around the world who wish to copy wealthy Americans, want white, white teeth. The dissatisfaction with natural tooth color, natural hair color, natural skin color, natural hair distribution, and normal body shape is an interesting human phenomenon.

Every such trend, or *culture change*, for which we have historical evidence, is initiated by someone and gradually spreads. The ubiquitous media have sped up this process. Advertising and marketing people know this and employ well-known celebrities to introduce and endorse their products. Scientific and medical evidence demonstrate many popular practices to be ill advised when considering our long-term health, but these data are ignored. People want to fit in, be hip, cool, gnarly, phat, sweet, real—terms used in various recent decades to describe conformity to popular societal behaviors.

Field studies of *Macaca fuscata,* the Japanese macaque monkey, demonstrate that a new behavior starts with young individuals, often females. It is then typically adopted in turn by young age-group cohorts, followed by adult females and males. The most famous example of this took place on Koshima Island where primatologists were conducting long-term studies of Japanese macaque behavior. Researchers placed piles of sweet potatoes on the beach daily. One day they observed a young female carry her sweet potato into the water and wash and then eat it—a behavior repeated as she ate. Researchers hypothesized that she was washing sand off of the potato and possibly seasoning her potato with the salty sea water. On subsequent days it was noticed that other juveniles began washing their potatoes, too. Finally adults began the process. It is documented that much of human innovative behavior—dress, types of body modification, and values—change within a group in the same sequence. It is an interesting comparison to ponder. Am I suggesting that there is something in our primate genetic heritage that causes this? Perhaps, but one must always remember that correlation doesn't always mean causation. It may just be random coincidence. Nonetheless it is interesting.

Research shows that people have been focusing on the appearance of their teeth for centuries. Archaeologists have uncovered evidence from the culture of the Maya, who lived in Mexico and Central America, of various ways they drew attention to the teeth—particularly as evidence of high social status. One Maya fresco depicts the process of drilling incisor teeth to inlay jade (the most popular material), quartz, turquoise, obsidian, and other stones. Evidence of numerous tooth customs is found on skeletons recovered in archaeological excavations from cultures around the world, and many of these customs are practiced today. In parts of Africa, for example, the filing of incisor teeth to points or incising marks on the buccal (cheek side) of incisors provides aesthetic focus, as does the ablation (removal) of incisor teeth. Many other cultures also have long traditions of tooth filing. In some places it is still popular and often reported as undertaken for aesthetic reasons, but it is also associated with various spiritual traditions. There is a recent trend in North America for people to request that their dentist file the point of their canine teeth flat, to be in line with the incisors. The result gives a nice, even tooth row, but to me this cultural fad results in teeth than look like my grandpa's false teeth. Canines are part of us as a species and speak of times in the distant past when they were used to pierce the skin of tough fruits. This opinion is, of course, coming from an anthropologist!

Examples of cultural values regarding tooth and gum color can be found in many cultures. There is a tradition of purposefully dying teeth black among the Kammu and other cultures of Laos, Vietnam, and Southeast Asia. This is achieved by several applications of a dye prepared from a mixture of resin (made from the secretions of insects that suck on tree sap), soot, and other ingredients, plus iron or copper. This treatment gives teeth a black shiny look. Shiny black smiles were considered beautiful by a majority of people in past generations, although this is changing. Tooth staining was in some societies part of a rite of passage. A *rite of passage* is a ritual that occurs as an individual moves from one social role and status to another within a culture. For example a marriage ritual is a rite of passage. Tooth staining was sometimes done as part of a ceremony associated with reaching adulthood. Some of these cultures explained their preference for black teeth by saying that only demons, animals, and savages have white teeth. There were also periods when black teeth were a status symbol, as was the case for a period of time in Japan. Gums are a focus of color alterations in other world cultures where a tattooing agent is applied to gums to change their color to black or blue-black.

There is a recent fashion among African Americans of placing gold caps on the incisor (front) teeth—usually the lateral incisors or canines—for aesthetic reasons or pride in belonging to this ethnic group. Some of these caps are made of solid gold, white gold, silver, or platinum, while others have cutout designs in the metal. One can go online and purchase inexpensive fake caps. Or, one can spend more money and purchase a mold kit: make a mold of your teeth at home, return the mold, and receive single caps or grills, made from materials you've chosen, with cutouts often done for free (inlays of jewels cost more). You receive them by return mail.

As noted previously, data abound, showing that a new custom associated with body adornment nearly always begins with those in the limelight of a culture or subculture. Crowns, caps, extensions (popular for applying to the canine teeth), and grills (also known as grillz or fronts) began with rap stars and the practice has trickled down and is now being copied by others. Rappers and musicians such as Li'l Wayne and Kanye

71

West helped to usher (note: I couldn't resist using this word here) in the popularity of grills. Grills are appliances that are more expensive than crowns and caps, and they typically cover several teeth such as from canine to canine on the mandible. Some are made of gold or platinum, and diamonds or other jewels sometimes encrust the grills. Grills fit over the teeth and can be worn for social events or performances and then removed at home, school, or the professional workplace. Anthropologists who have studied the crown and grill phenomena say that while they are often worn for aesthetic reasons, they are also a sign of high social *status* and wealth. It has also been suggested that they signal the opposite sex that this person is wealthy and therefore a desirable sexual partner.

The popularity of white teeth is not new! Among ancient Romans goat milk and urine were used to clean and whiten teeth, and there are many variations on these techniques noted in historical records and in contemporary cultures. I recall as a child my mother offering baking soda (an abrasive) to clean tooth stains caused by eating blackberries. And I've heard of people putting mashed up strawberry pulp (it contains a mild acid) on tooth surfaces for a few minutes to clean stains. The current popularity of teeth whitening by bleaching began in the 1990s, and it is a common practice today.

Contemporary teeth whitening takes several forms. First there is *teeth whitening* that, according to the FDA, simply restores natural color to the teeth. These whitening agents remove *surface stains* through mild abrasives and chemical or polishing agents. Most whitening toothpastes use this approach, and it is the one used throughout human history. Next, there are various *bleaching* techniques. These can actually change the color of the tooth enamel. At-home bleaching of tooth enamel typically involves peroxide-containing whiteners in a gel placed in a mouth guard for a period of time (different products involve various regimens). Finally, there are professional whitening procedures done by a dentist. These involve a bleaching agent that is applied to the teeth using various shields to protect the mouth's soft tissues. Special lights or even lasers are then used that work with the whitening agents. As my hygienist noted, and I found in my research, some individuals want to get their teeth whiter and whiter. There is an actual name for this—bleachorexia—obsessing over the color of one's teeth in an unhealthy way.

The culturally created focus on tooth beauty is certainly interesting to ponder. In an age when you celebrate your ability to make independent choices, do you stop to consider the very real and *powerful* influence culture and subculture have on the "choices" you make? Why do you focus on having white teeth, not merely healthy clean teeth? Why should beautiful teeth be white, instead of black, red, or gold? Do you give thought to *why* you may want whiter teeth?

Challenge: Ponder and try to pinpoint how you acquired your attitude about the color of your teeth. What aspects of the enculturation process were at work?

Thinking It Through
- Describe examples of cross-cultural modification of tooth color.
- Discuss techniques used to change the color of teeth.

Anthropological Terms

culture	rite of passage
culture change	status
enculturation	

Thinking Practically
- Identify three aspects of how humans learn their culture that are at work in the white-teeth fad.
- Defend the custom of decorating incisor teeth with inlaid jewels or the wearing of a grill.
- Look on the internet at red-carpet photos from a recent major celebrity event such as the Academy Awards. Focus on the teeth of the celebrities. Describe the variation you note in the appearance of their teeth. Compare this to the variation you see in photos of your Facebook friends or classmates.

10 ~ Fireballs

*Rituals both sacred and secular, together with the encultura-
tion of values, are found in all world cultures and microcultures. Examples of secular rituals grab the author's attention
at a regional swim meet, and she reflects on these behaviors
from tribal to contemporary times.*

It is a bright sunny morning with a mere whisper of a breeze, just enough
to unfurl Old Glory flying high at the competition venue. The clamor of
voices creates a festive atmosphere. Pop-up canopies in a multitude of colors—green, red, yellow, blue, red and blue stripes, yellow and blue stripes—
crowd the grassy areas adjacent to, but just outside, the wrought-iron fence
surrounding the Olympic size swimming pool. Banners bright with team
colors and logos showing images of mascots—Fireballs, Aqua Bears, Sharks,
Dolphins, Sunsets, Electric Eels, Barracudas—proclaim the territory of
each of the Valley Swim League's summer recreational swim teams. This
morning is the end of summer championship meet. Under the pop-ups are
beach chairs, of the folding variety, most with arm rests and holders for
water bottles or drink cans, plus rugs, towels, or blankets for people who
want to sit on the ground or lie down to rest. Large picnic coolers and folding tables hold drinks and snacks for athletes and their supporters.

Snatches of conversations are heard as young people scurry past: "She
should be able to lap her Shark competitor?" "I just want to not finish
last." "We can win this." A coach is intensely conversing with a young

swimmer and demonstrates arm movements for the backstroke in exaggerated slow motion, perhaps to correct a style flaw he noted in this morning's practice laps. A parent says to his son, "Your hours of practice and hard work have earned you a spot on the team. Now go out there, give it your all, and have fun." Such encouraging words abound.

My granddaughter Katherine is a member of the Fireballs team, and I am caught up in the anticipatory excitement surrounding me. At the same time, I contemplate the mascot images and think about why they may have been chosen. Each symbolizes and expresses strength, speed, agility, or dominance. The Fireballs' mascot, for example, is the image of a spectacular, green ball with large swim goggle–clad eyes and a provocative grin; it spews colorful gold and red flames that flicker in the wake of the speeding ball slicing through water. The Sharks' mascot is a fierce looking shark with a big tooth-baring smile and a piercing gaze. The Dolphins' mascot is depicted by two dolphins leaping in an arc out of the water.

Just as Katherine hurries off to participate in the tradition of her team's pre-meet cheer, I think *ritual* and flashes of ritual events from world cultures (and the theoretical comparisons of and explanations for them) march through my memory; my anthropological perspective is always with me. *Ritual* is behavior that is regularly repeated, is formalized, has symbolic content, and is often used to bond members of a group. While specific definitions may vary somewhat, these features are usually included. Most people hearing the word "ritual" think of religion; it is often used as an analytical tool in this context. The term is also used, however, to describe and analyze everyday secular behaviors. Note: as with all aspects of culture there may be variation in both how individuals perceive rituals and perform them, yet group members recognize the behaviors as rituals. Many who observe a person performing a ritual behavior will call it a superstition—a false implication that the repeated behavior can cause a desired outcome.

Categories of ritual ceremonies found in world cultures include rites of intensification and rites of passage. **Rites of intensification** place emphasis on an entire group of people—a culture, subculture, or microculture. Features of these rites may include rituals that reinforce (1) values of the group, (2) the solidarity of the group, and (3) status relationships, both social and political, within the group. I'll look for these features as the swim meet unfolds. Solidarity, for example, is apparent and reinforced by team members wearing jackets, swimsuits, and caps bearing team logos plus gathering together to give their team cheer before the meet begins. I make a mental note to explain the concept of ritual to Katherine and ask her (at a later time) to give me her analysis of the event.

Rites of passage (and the rituals associated with them) mark a biological or social phase in an individual's life—birth, puberty, coming of age, adulthood, graduation, marriage, death. An individual is the focus of a rite of passage and its associated rituals; the group to which that person belongs is also involved as the group focuses attention on the individual. Changes in an individual's expectations and behaviors result from his or her new social *role* and *status*. Members of his or her group will also, in the future, relate differently toward the individual. There is comfort in performing such traditional rituals. In team sport participation individuals may experience a rite of passage as they move from a junior team to a senior team or from a recreational team to a professional team.

Rituals in the form of superstitious behaviors abound in the sports world and in behaviors practiced by people every day as well. Such behaviors have psychological benefits for individuals who perform them. Rituals of this type have no actual connection to any outcome but make athletes feel more confident. What could it hurt if he or she always repeats a behavior prior to an event? Australia's ace Olympic swimmer Stephanie Rice always did eight arm swings, four goggle presses, and four cap touches before she took her mark on the starting blocks. The United States swimmer Michael Phelps, holder of 23 Olympic gold medals, followed specific warm up rituals as well. These included stepping up on the starting block, stepping off of the starting block, swinging his arms three times, stepping back on the starting block, and getting into start position.

The Western world's awareness of the commonality of ritual across cultures began when anthropologists started reporting on their fieldwork experiences in the 1860s. Anthropologists have always held that a benefit of learning about "others" (other cultures) is that one begins to know and understand more about one's own culture. This was underscored repeatedly as they wrote about the tribal world. It continues as current anthropologists observe, study, and share their data on issues such as poverty, inequality, and war in contemporary world societies. Today's social media and information on the internet continue to bring this lesson to people in all cultures.

Bronislaw Malinowski's ethnographic work with the Trobriand Islanders provides the classic example of the role and function of ritual in people's lives. Malinowski lived among Trobrianders for several years, longer than most fieldworkers. He was isolated there during World War I, resulting in a very detailed look at another culture from an outsider's perspective (often today termed an *etic view*). He attempted to also describe how the Trobrianders themselves thought about issues (termed an *emic view*).

A major focus of Malinowski's work was magic and belief, topics that Western cultures were curious about at that time. For example, he examined the use of magic ritual in fishing activities. When embarking on an expedition out to dangerous open seawater, fishermen followed several rituals and were anxious to perform them correctly. They believed the rituals kept them safe and improved their catch. In the safer, reef protected waters of the inner lagoon they didn't carry out any rituals.

When observing an athlete perform a ritual before a sporting event, I usually think of Malinowski's descriptions. Yesterday, when watching football's Super Bowl 50 with my husband, I smiled as one team's quarterback (caught on camera) folded his hands, bowed his head, and said a brief prayer (*sacred ritual*). He then kissed his finger, removed it from his lips, and pointed the finger outward and up. A television commentator informed us that he was sending a kiss to his mother (a personal, *secular ritual*); he had followed these rituals, asking both God's and his mother's blessings, before each game since he played in high school. Rituals performed by athletes such as the kiss to his mother, a baseball pitcher tugging three times on his cap before pitching ball, or a hockey player twirling his stick and tapping the ice, begin when a player makes a connection, however illogical, between winning and losing a game. When the ritual is perceived to work most times and one is successful the behavior becomes ritualized. Malinowski reported that the Trobriand fishermen could recall a poor catch or a disaster that occurred when someone didn't do one of the open sea fishing rituals. Of course, one can correctly note that they knew it was safer to go out fishing in good weather so they avoided going out when the sea was rough; still they felt it was, as we might say, "better to be safe than sorry" so they always did the ritual. Inuit hunters of Northern Canada performed specific rituals associated with seal hunting aimed at appeasing Sedna, a sea goddess who was considered to have once been a young Inuit woman and then transformed to a goddess upon her death. Specific acts such as offering a ritual drink of water to a seal before butchering it were believed to ensure that Sedna would continue to send seals to the Inuit. A hunter who did not perform a traditional ritual was later blamed for a downturn in Inuit hunting.

Ritual is also found in many everyday situations. I clearly recall one of my students who came to class, bluebook in hand, ready for the big test. Suddenly she frantically began looking through her backpack. She appeared near tears. When I inquired what the problem was she nearly shouted that she could not take the test. I asked why. She looked right at me and said she had studied for the test and felt she knew the material, but she couldn't find her lucky pen in her backpack. She had to use that specific pen to write her exam. She was terribly stressed. I told her to go out and look in her car and return. She did. Ten minutes later she walked into the room holding a pen and had a big "found it" smile on her face. She aced that exam. She later told me, in all seriousness, that she had gotten A's on every test she took with that pen. Using it to write her exams had become a personal ritual (regularly, repeated behavior) for her.

There is a swirl of activity around me and it is difficult for me to focus on being the anthropological me, so I make mental note of a few observations and go on to enjoy the swim event.

Katherine informs me she is competing today in the girls 15- to 18-year-old age group 200-meter medley relay for the Fireballs. She is 10. The

79

Fireballs team has very few swimmers in the older age category and none are particularly fast in the freestyle stroke. Not wanting to forfeit the event or place last, and thus miss out on important overall team points, the Fireballs coach has assigned her to swim the anchor leg of the relay. This discretionary substitution is allowed under the meet rules and allows a team to earn participation points. Overall points (participation plus finish times in each event) count in determining the meet's overall winning team. The coach knows that this young girl has a great team spirit and attitude besides being a fast freestyle swimmer. So, she is taking one for the team rather than being placed in the freestyle event for her age group. I reflect on this American value that is reinforced over and over in kids' sports (part of the enculturation process). And I am filled with pride at such a mature outlook on Katherine's part (I, too, am a product of my culture!).

When the call comes for swimmers in the 15- to 18-year-old medley relay, the spectators can see the four girls from each team line up behind the starting blocks in each of the seven lanes of the pool. All of the participants tower over my petite granddaughter. The order of the strokes in this event is backstroke, breaststroke, butterfly, and freestyle (each girl swims 50 meters). The starting whistle blows and the race begins. Her teammates do well in the backstroke and breaststroke but fall behind in the butterfly. The Fireballs are in last place.

Katherine steps onto the block. Her size compared to the other six teams' freestyle swimmers standing on the blocks is visually stunning. A parent behind me in the stands loudly remarks: "Look at that little girl swimming the anchor leg for the Fireballs." As her Fireballs teammate swimming the butterfly touches the pool wall (still in last place), Katherine explodes off the block and into the water. She surfaces and with her flawless, efficient stroke and kick she swims. At the 25-meter turn she is still a bit behind the current sixth-place swimmer from a competing team, but Katherine is quickly closing the gap between them. Inch by inch she moves up after a textbook perfect turn at 25 meters. Our family joins the clamor of shouted encouragement from Fireballs fans. In the last five meters she surges ahead to finish sixth and earn valuable team points for the Fireballs. I'm cheering and on my feet as her team surrounds and congratulates her. And I think, wow this is certainly enculturation at work. Later as I hug and congratulate her in celebration of her finish, she remarks that she is very pleased with her swim (her time was her personal best) and the fact that she didn't finish last, thus enhancing the team's chance to win the overall championship since they are very strong in other events.

Later, I discussed the idea of ritual with Katherine (she is accustomed to me looking at things anthropologically; I'm looking for an insider's viewpoint, too). She immediately began to tell me about how a swim meet unfolds and pointed out what she thought fit my explanation of ritual behavior. She said one ritual is the order of pre-meet warm-up swims—the oldest team members always warm up in the pool first, followed in descending order by each swimmer's age. Older experienced members are respected and have higher status. After the warm-up all team members gather around their coach for their pre-meet team cheer. She said she thinks this and wearing clothing (especially swim caps) with the team logo creates team spirit and bonds the team. There is a strictly followed order to the meet events. I asked whether there are ritualized behaviors by the individual swimmers before they compete in their events. I had observed lots of arm swinging, cap pulling, and goggle touching, but since this was my first meet I didn't know if these were individual member's rituals or were random behaviors. She replied that some swimmers always touch the pool side or always readjust their goggles or do so a specific number of times, but she doesn't do that. Several days later she tells me that in the end the Fireballs lost both the meet and the season league overall championship to the Dolphins, but they are pleased with league second place and they will work harder next season to win the league championship.

Where do you observe everyday behavior that is ritualized?

Challenge: Describe details of two secular ritual behaviors participated in by students.

Thinking It Through

• Wear your anthropological analytical lenses the next time you are at or participate in a sporting event. List and describe three rituals participated in by a team or a team member.

• Discuss two functions of secular ritual behavior. Discuss how the rituals create solidarity and reinforce group identity.

• What was the function of the "lucky pen ritual" for the author's student? Describe a ritual that you or a friend performs before exams or in athletic events.

Anthropological Terms

emic	role
etic	sacred ritual
rite of intensification	secular ritual
rite of passage	status
ritual	

Thinking Practically

• If you were assigned to coach a kids' baseball or soccer team discuss how introducing a couple of rituals into team practices could be beneficial to the group.

• You have just been hired to head a team at your workplace. Are there any secular rituals you might suggest to the team to promote cohesiveness? How could you do this?

11 ~ Return of the Kitchen Elf

Supernatural beings are an integral part of cultural belief systems, both religious and secular. Details are varied and rich. All such beliefs function within cultures, and for individual members of cultures, in similar ways. Several everyday beliefs and their functions are explored with a focus on the author's kitchen elf.

A clink, a small scream followed by tears, and a river of milk spread across the kitchen table and dripped on the floor. Again. My small daughter had been experiencing a run of such disasters. My husband and I generally dealt with them by reminding her that she needed to be careful and pay attention when she reached for something. It was clear that she was becoming stressed by these events that seemed to happen almost daily. I looked at her sad face as she said it was an accident and she would try harder, and on impulse I said, "Don't worry about it, honey, mommy has figured out what is causing these accidents." The crying stopped and she looked at me expectantly. As I mopped up the mess I went on, "I think that we have an elf living in our kitchen. And for some reason this elf is a trickster who thinks it is fun to cause people difficulties." I launched into a mini-anthropological lecture on the topic telling her that trickster beings are found in many cultures and often, it seems, they only want attention.

I now had her full attention. I explained that if we acknowledged the kitchen elf, and perhaps left a treat out for him occasionally, he might stop moving the glass so that it easily tipped over. We talked some more and she asked questions about where he might live and why we couldn't see him and what he might look like. Then she announced, while giving me a serious, somber look, she thought I was right.

The next time we were at the table, her napkin fell off of her lap. As she got down from the chair to retrieve it she said, "I think the kitchen elf pulled my napkin off of my lap." My husband and I exchanged a look and both agreed. And so it was that the kitchen elf took up residence in our kitchen and was blamed for a variety of accidents. Over a period of two weeks the spilled-milk accidents declined and then stopped altogether. The elf was still blamed if a spoon was dropped or a napkin fell, but that, too, stopped after a few weeks.

Several months later we were gathering ingredients for making chocolate chip cookies. I was measuring flour and my daughter opened the refrigerator to get an egg. I heard a splat and looked to see the broken egg lying on the floor. As I was about to say something about being more careful, my daughter said, "Uh-oh. Mom. It looks like the kitchen elf is back." And what could I say to that! Smart kid. The elf appeared from time to time when there were minor mishaps in the kitchen.

Supernatural beings are part of supernatural belief systems the world over. *Supernaturalism* may be defined as belief in anything beyond the natural world—beings and objects and happenings that cannot be scientifically tested and proven to exist. All people divide the world into the natural and the supernatural, although that dividing line differs between cultures.

Supernatural beings include deities (gods, goddesses—some are all-powerful, others reign over specific areas or activities), souls, ghosts, witches, and *tricksters*, to name the most common ones. A feature of supernatural beings is that they have human attributes, both good and bad, such as greed, love, desire, jealousy, cleverness, and cruelty; they are moral, immoral, virtuous, scheming, and so forth.

Trickster beings make mischief; they play tricks on people to amuse themselves. They are contradictory—sometimes they are good, sometimes they are bad. Some tricksters are responsible for creating or helping create the world. Major tricksters in some cultures are responsible for creating or helping create particular elements such as fire. Minor tricksters might steal food or trip you so that you drop and break something you are carrying. Tricksters are described in some of the first cross-cultural *ethnographies* that describe fieldwork carried out by anthropologists in the latter part of the nineteenth century. Tricksters are still found today in contemporary cultures. Some cultures have several trickster beings; others have only one. Tales are told and retold about tricksters, and these stories become part of the enculturation process of a culture.

There are entire books written about tricksters such as Coyote and Raven in Native American cultures and the trickster Spider in West African cultures. For example, events like losing possessions, failure or success in hunting, and an accidental injury were blamed on Coyote (a major trickster of central and western North America) or explained by his interference. Raven, a Pacific Northwest trickster, created land and lured (or released, in some tales) people from a large clamshell on a beach, and he gave them fire and light. He also was at times mischievous, and he was always hungry and often tricked other animals to get his food. In West Africa, Anansi the trickster is a spider about whom there is a complex and rich history of tales recounting his activities, from creating the sun and moon to tricking people so that he can steal money or food.

The trickster category of supernatural beings is complicated and multifaceted. It has been widely analyzed and interpreted, from both *emic* (insider) and *etic* (outsider) perspectives. Anthropologists as well as those who study mythology in literature have written widely about the subject. What all of the analyses come down to is that many tricksters provide *a foil for explaining why people are not perfect and for explaining the state of the world and why it is not perfect—blame can be laid on tricksters*. Other tricksters help explain bad luck and good luck. Typically stories of tricksters are repeated to children, and they are often told that certain ritual behaviors (leaving food, providing a container of water in the garden, speaking to them in certain locations) will dispose the tricksters to be good to them. For example, on the Isle of Man off of the west coast of England, the local

Manx people would regularly voice greetings to the *mooinjer veggey* (the local name of an Isle of Man trickster) as they crossed the Ballalonna Bridge located on the Castletown-Douglas road. My friend, who was born and raised there, says children and adults always said *moghrey mie* (good morning), *fastye mie* (good afternoon), or *oie vie* (good night), or just gave a hand wave to salute the little people when the humans crossed over the "Fairy Bridge." Not to do so would bring bad luck. If you talked to the fairies as you crossed, they would bring you good luck.

I have relatives who live in Hawaii. They insist that little people—called *menehune*—live on the islands. They are seldom seen, are active at night, and often hassle people, although they can be helpful too. The *menehune* live in the mountain highlands. They are small (two to three feet tall) and hairy. My relatives had a personal experience with these tricksters when returning in the early evening from a day in Honolulu to find the kitchen sink plugged by a paper towel, the faucet on, and the water overflowing from the sink. One of their children said that he'd seen bushes near the house moving as they drove up the driveway (presumably the *menehune* making their escape). The family resumed their practice of leaving an occasional treat outside for the *menehune*, and they had no more incidents.

Menehune legends abound in Hawaii and are often complex. Should you visit Hawaii you will encounter many such legends. As with other oral traditions, stories about them alter and are embellished over time. Like many tricksters, they can also be helpful—the large Alekoko fishpond near Lihue on the island of Kauai, for example, is attributed to having been built by the *menehune* in just one night! Archaeologists have determined that the fishpond was created 800 years ago and is now on the *National Register of Historic Places*.

The leprechauns of Ireland were considered fairy folk who were mischievous and liked to play jokes and pranks (qualifying them as tricksters). I once discussed leprechauns with a colleague who is Irish. I asked about beliefs he experienced as a youngster, trying to place these beings in a functionalist's model of supernaturalism that I was then lecturing on.

After a brief general discussion, he confided in me that his great success in the stock market was due to the advice of his personal leprechaun whom he chatted with regularly. This man was a serious scholar, and he imparted this information to me in confidence. I was unable to tell if he was joking, but I thought it would be outstanding to have such an advisor (everyone at the college knew of his investment successes).

The overarching functions of all belief systems, as seen from the outside, is that they *explain* happenings that are unexplainable—why things happen, where we come from, where we go when we die. Specific functions have been described as falling within categories—social functions, psychological functions, and ecological functions. Social functions help groups of people; psychological functions help both individuals and groups; ecological functions contribute in positive ways to the environment.

My husband and I (he is also an anthropologist) like to summarize these functions more specifically with the acronym CREEDS. "C" stands for cohesive, meaning that belief systems hold people who share beliefs together. Believers experience ceremonies and ritual celebrations together and know that they are not alone. "R" stands for revitalizing, meaning that values are renewed with each repeat of prayers, songs, or stories relating to the supernatural. "E" stands for several functions—how beliefs *explain* happenings and people's history, how belief systems *educate* people about their culture and history, how people feel good or even "high," *euphoric*, when they participate in rituals and share beliefs, and some beliefs have *ecological* functions by directing people as to how they should treat the Earth. "D" stands for the *disciplining* function of belief systems—where the belief system prescribes a specific activity or behavior among the practitioners. An excellent example would be the Judeo-Christian dictums known as the Ten Commandments. A similar set of disciplinary guidelines can also be found in the Koran/Quran of Islam, sometimes called the Ten Instructions. Likewise, Hinduism has a set of Ten Disciplines that outline proper behavior for the believers. Finally, "S" stands for the *supportive* function of belief systems—people who hold common beliefs support and aid each other emotionally, politically, and economically.

The trickster Coyote mentioned above provided primarily an explanatory function within aboriginal North American cultures. I've thought of blaming him when I can't find my car keys or cell phone, instead of taking responsibility for misplacing them. Also, if those around me held this belief in Coyote then they would accuse *him* rather than pointing out my inattentiveness in misplacing or losing the keys or phone. This would be supportive for me and I've wondered if it would lower my blood pressure and stress level. Would all of us feel better if we could, in psychological terms, rationalize such losses? Would blaming tricksters for small mishaps, such as the spilled milk in my kitchen, reduce anger levels or at least redirect it away from ourselves? Hmm. . . .

The kitchen elf fits well into the explanatory function of beliefs. It gives a reason for something happening and directs the blame away from a person or group. This elf serves both individuals (my daughter, my husband, and I) and our group (in this case our household). We all feel better, perhaps not euphoric but certainly, for my daughter, relieved. Child psychologists might frown on my blaming that elf for the spilt milk, but it worked for my family.

Return of the kitchen elf: Fast-forward to a recent family dinner. My four-year-old grandson bumped his milk glass and over it went. As the "be more careful" admonitions and "that's the third time this week" were voiced around the table, Mamu (me) chimed in with, "Oh dear, I believe you have a kitchen elf in your house." I looked at my daughter and she smiled and immediately consoled her young son that, indeed, it appeared that there was a kitchen elf creating "trouble" for the family. He listened intently as she told him of the difficulties that the elf used to cause her. In a few weeks the spilt milk problem ceased. Kids are smart; my grandson, like his mother before him, "got" the efficacy and understood the functions of believing in this little supernatural being. Now when minor mishaps occur in the kitchen or dining room we suddenly hear my granddaughter or grandson blame it on the kitchen elf.

Challenge: Consider a supernatural being within your culture. How does belief in this being function to aid individuals? How does it function for the society as a whole?

Thinking It Through

- Identify types of beliefs in supernatural beings found across cultures.
- Explain and discuss the functions of supernatural beliefs within cultures.

Anthropological Terms

emic	supernatural beings
ethnographies	supernaturalism
etic	tricksters

Thinking Practically

- Identify two supernatural beings within your culture that serve an explanatory function for the society. Compare the features of these beings with ones that you have read about in an ethnographic account of another culture.
- Describe the supernatural beings believed in by small children in North American culture. How do they function and why do adults perpetuate the belief in them?
- Identify two supernatural beings created for Hollywood films and discuss their functions within the films.

12 ~ We Are the Eagles

Early anthropological ethnographers often wrote of totemism when describing belief systems of aboriginal cultures. The author explores the concept when, through her anthropological lens, she finds aspects of the practice in a local elementary school.

San Francisco 49er quarterback Colin Kaepernick of the National Football League had just thrown another successful pass resulting in a touchdown. That pass completion ended the National Football Conference playoffs and sent the San Francisco 49ers to the Super Bowl to play against the American Football Conference Ravens of Baltimore. The crowd at the stadium, as they say, went wild! Cameras transmitting from local sports bars in Northern California showed crowds of red-and-gold-clad fans shouting and cheering. The team colors are part of the symbolic package of the 49er team. Interviews with fans followed. One man attending the game said that he is a second-generation 49er fan; a woman said 49er fans are the best. The sports announcer made a short aside about the loyalty of the 49er booster clubs, known as the Niner's Nation. I was curious about the number of such clubs and their locations, so I Googled it. I was surprised to find that, besides the many clubs in Northern California, there are clubs all across the United States and in other countries.

My husband remarked how team names (Bears, Lions, Falcons, Dolphins, Patriots, Wolverines, and 49ers) or team mascots function as symbolic totems within contemporary society and I agreed. As anthropologists we have conversations like this frequently. Our comparisons of aspects of contemporary North American society with those of world cultures is ongoing in our lives and makes for some interesting conversations (and, I admit, some disagreements). Details may differ, but there are many commonalities among cultures, particularly regarding the functions of symbols such as team names and mascots.

I recalled thinking about totems last fall when collecting my granddaughter from school. "I am an Eagle," she announced at the end of her first day of kindergarten. "An eager Eagle." She went on to tell me that her friend Anna, who was in another class, was a Toucan; another friend was a Frog. She explained that each kindergarten class was an animal, and she and her classmates would be Eagles "forever." This form of organization by class makes sense—the kids build on this theme all year. It unites and defines them. The Eagles are eager; the Toucans are terrific; the Frogs are fantastic, and so on. They take pride in belonging and are loyal to others in their class. And Eagles can soar—her repeated use of this word in her description suggested to me that a new vocabulary word was added to that of all Eagles on this day. The next week when I picked her up after school, I found the walls outside of her classroom covered in the classes' drawings. Eagles were flying, soaring, standing on nests, and catching fish in their talons. All of the birds had white heads, dark bodies and wings, and were portrayed in a clear blue sky. They had been learning about eagles. The eagle, in anthropological terms, was the *totem* of this class of 20 children.

Totemism is a concept that refers to a *symbolic* association of animals, plants, and sometimes objects or geographic locations with a group of people—identifying them *at a level above ordinary kinship or other group relationships*. Totems connect people to nature as well as to each other emotionally. In the tribal world totemism is commonly associated with kinship groups such as clans. A *clan* is a kin group consisting of two or more lineages; a *lineage* is a kin group that traces its bloodline through males or females. In large tribal societies there are typically several clans. Each clan traces its origin to a common mythical tribal totem ancestor. The mythical animal may have created everything on Earth and in the heavens, including begetting or revealing the first human members of the clan.

Totemism in aboriginal culture was identified early in nineteenth-century anthropological research. At first it was received by peoples of Western societies as a curiosity and ethnocentrically considered a part of "primitive" tribal cultures. The use of the term "primitive" at this time was a part of Western "civilized" peoples' implicit belief that non-Western peoples were lower down on the ladder of cultural evolution. Theories about totemism became connected to this idea—in the works of Edward B. Tylor, for example. He and others made hypotheses about the *evolutionary* sequence of human culture based on various criteria. The word primitive was used in some of these evolutionary schemes; others used terms such as "savagery" and "barbarism"—anthropology was reflecting the general perception Western cultures held for aboriginal, non-Western cultures.

Anthropology grew and matured as a behavioral science and the *functionalist perspective* became popular. As theories shifted, totemism was viewed as a belief that "functioned" to unite members of a society for the common good (e.g., this is depicted in the work of A. R. Radcliffe-Brown) or to psychologically provide individuals with the security that often comes with group membership (e.g., as seen in the work of B. Malinowski). Both Radcliffe-Brown and Malinowski were influential alpha males in the development of anthropology in the early twentieth century. Émile Durkheim (1915), who wrote what is now considered a classic study of religion, thought that totems represented a type of symbolism, and he described at length the totem clans of the Australian aboriginal peoples.

The facts of totemic beliefs continue to be shared and vigorously debated by scholars. Issues such as how totems arose and why they were chosen are discussed—e.g., were they sacred because they were important to the society and its well-being (e.g., a food source) or were they chosen on whim and over time became sacred? As with all theories of origins of human customs, we will never know. Such issues, however, make for engaging intellectual debates, and I think it is interesting that an argument can be made for the existence of forms of totemism in contemporary societies.

In most *tribes*, clan totems create relationships between several lineages. Because clans follow *exogamous* rules (ones that specify which group you must marry outside of), a person's mother and father belong to different clans. A culture's descent rules determine whether a person inherits the totem from the mother or the father. So if you picture a society made up of totemic clans you see a web of people connected to each other. I must tell you that not all totemic clans have these exogamous rules, attesting yet again to the diversity of human culture.

Cross-cultural totemic beliefs may be classified into several categories, such as kinship-based totems (e.g., a clan may adopt a specific totem); locality-based totems (a totem associated with a person's place of birth or where they live); and *moiety*-based totems (when a society, especially tribes, are divided into two groups, such as female and male, with each sex having its own totem). I would add school-affiliated totems and athletic-team totems. All function in one major way—they create group solidarity by identifying and connecting individuals—like the people that identify with the San Francisco 49ers.

When I first started thinking about totems after learning about the Eagles, I knew I wasn't the first to think of group symbols or mascots in this way. Sure enough, I located anthropologist Ralph Linton's analysis of totemism in the United States Army during World War I. He published his analysis in an article entitled "Totemism and the A.E.F.," which appeared in the journal *American Anthropologist* in 1924. Linton describes the example of the growth of a *totem-like* complex in the 42nd Division of the United States Army during World War I. The division was given the name "Rainbow" because it consisted of a variety of regiments, and each had different regimental colors that reminded some higher-up official of the colors of a rainbow. The name was infrequently used while the 42nd was in the United States, but after they arrived in France it was used more and more frequently. It became a source of division solidarity, and soldiers identified themselves as Rainbows when they met individuals outside of the division. The appearance of a rainbow was considered a good omen. Rainbows began to be painted on military objects. Soon other military units began to adopt mascots; again, these functioned to promote group solidarity.

Linton notes how a member of an Australian aboriginal clan would refer to himself as a kangaroo or other animal. He saw a parallel with the soldiers who would say to a stranger, "I'm a Rainbow." Athletic-team members and fans can be heard today to refer to themselves in this way. Consider, for example, the Boston Bruins—a team in the National Hockey League—a bruin is an animal with speed and agility, or the Toronto Blue Jays—a Major League Baseball team—a blue jay is a bird that is aggressive and strong. College alumni do this, too—referring to themselves by the school mascot name. Think of the University of Michigan Wolverines—a wolverine is tenacious and tough. Increasingly elementary school classes have similar totem-like symbols that help create group solidarity.

Nowadays, no one thinks of these named, contemporary groups as having the symbol of an ancestor, even a mythical one; we don't have prohibitions about whom we can marry based on which team we support. However, we do cite characteristics of these totemic representations and assign these to members of the "totem" group. What characteristics are assigned to team totems such as Ravens, Falcons, and Dolphins? Some mascots, such as the "Banana Slug," the mascot of The University of California at Santa Cruz, or the Stanford University "Tree," or The University of Notre Dame "Leprechaun," may not fit the label "totem" quite as neatly as others (although the slug and the tree are part of nature) but still function to *create solidarity* among students and alumni. The next time you watch an athletic-team event listen for characteristics associated with the team name being cited as responsible for aspects of the team's performance (e.g., "The Warriors are fierce competitors").

Grade schools that create totem associations for children's classes are, of course, groups without any biological connection. Close analysis, however, reveals that they also function in much the same manner as the mythical totem ancestor of tribal clans. Clan members have solidarity and emotional ties. Eagles are found at schools besides that of my granddaughter. A chance encounter with another Eagle while at a summer camp or on the beach is cause to reminisce and recount school experiences. A bond is discovered where there may be no other. One feels less alone or isolated. This is certainly the case among tribal peoples who, when meeting a stranger, often toss out questions about the other's clan or tribal affiliation. If a common totem can be established, then the other is not an adversary to be feared. Today, strangers often make queries of one another or offer information such as where one lives or one's university affiliation, job, hobbies, or favorite sport team. Supporting the same team, as in saying "I'm a Colts fan," creates a bond. This connection can serve to unite people and make them feel like acquaintances or even friends.

My granddaughter is now in first grade where the class is known as the Lions. The first-grade class is a mix of the four previous kindergarten classes: Eagles, Toucans, Turtles, and Frogs. Although the first-grade students separated themselves according to their kindergarten affiliations at the beginning of the school year, as their solidarity grew within the new class, and with the guidance of their teacher, they became Lions. The students now refer to themselves as Lions and speak of themselves as being fierce, brave, highly intelligent, and courageous. Still, I've heard my granddaughter identify her special friends as former Eagles or Frogs. So the initial "totem" affiliation continues even as they become part of a new affiliation. Multiple totems are not unusual in tribal societies where, for example, one may belong to the clan totem of one's birth and also belong to a sex-based totem, depending on whether one is male or female.

When viewed from an *etic* (outsider's) perspective, the contemporary examples discussed in this essay function in the same manner as tribal "totems," with perhaps two exceptions, as Ralph Linton noted with the 42nd Division Rainbows—they lack a belief in the common descent of members and they don't have any rules that regulate marriage (i.e., that a person has to marry within his or her own totem group, or that they must only marry a specified other totem group). Having said this, each football season one can overhear conversations where 49er fans joke that they can never marry a (fill in the blank) because they are a 49er!

Challenge: Can you name other affiliation groups in your community and throughout North America that use animals to identify their group?

Thinking It Through
- Explain the place of totemism in the belief systems of aboriginal cultures.
- Examine the contemporary occurrence and use of totemism.

Anthropological Terms

clan	moiety
etic	totem
exogamous	tribe
lineage	

Thinking Practically
- Defend the author's hypothesis that contemporary totems exist in the form of athletic-team mascots.
- Relate a personal experience you had when traveling where you and a stranger sought common backgrounds in your conversation (neither of you did this on purpose) and how you felt when one was discovered.
- What totems have you been associated with? Describe their characteristics and how you felt about being a member of this group.

13 ~ "I Do!"

The definition of marriage is an ongoing discussion within the United States—with both personal and political implications. In this essay marriage is discussed using anthropology's cross-cultural perspective that demonstrates marriage is a social construct as the author attends a neighbor's same-sex marriage celebration.

The cars have been arriving for three days as friends and family gather for today's event. My neighbor and her partner are getting married, and this festive ceremony has been in the works for months. When I saw her earlier this week she ran into the house and came back with a large envelope out of which she pulled their marriage license. The United States Supreme Court's ruling against California's controversial proposition banning same-sex marriage had been announced two days earlier. She and her partner were thrilled that they would be able to have, not just a commitment ceremony as originally planned, but a legal wedding.

Headlines, letters to the editor, social media, and personal conversations have focused on marriage and its definition. Everyone has an opinion of what marriage is and/or should be. This is strongly influenced by how one was **enculturated**. How do you define marriage?

Historical documentation shows that contemporary Western culture's idea *and* ideal of marriage—based on love, romance, and finding a soul mate—is fairly recent and not ubiquitous. Prior to about 150 years ago, marriage consisted of an event that mainly marked a change in an individual's role (the part a person plays in society) and status (a person's position in society). Today, in many cultures, status and role change is the focus of marriage.

When people marry they move from being single to being part of a couple and they acquire in-laws. This move gives them new rights and responsibilities within their group. Based on more than a century of anthropological data on the subject, we can say that in most societies marriage has the following features: (1) exclusive sexual relationship, (2) economic interdependency—contributing to labor and its rewards and property ownership for example, and (3) legitimacy of offspring and responsibility of raising them. I'm sure that you note here that I am not giving a definition of marriage, rather I am pointing out common cross-cultural features of what societies assign and expect from a married couple. These are not absolute features, and there are exceptions to each. For example, in some societies extramarital sex is accepted. In addition, as with many customs, there will always be the distinction between what is considered "ideal" behavior and what is "real" behavior. The current cultural debate finds many opposing views of what constitutes marriage. These are expressed daily in newspapers and on Facebook, Twitter, and other social media.

As a college freshman, I recall reading about the various forms that marriage takes, in addition to monogamy (defined in cross-cultural research as one man and one woman). Across cultures a man with more than one wife (*polygyny*) is the most popular form of marriage (keep in mind that this refers to a tabulation of cultures, not world population). Many wives means many workers (the wives and their children) to share labor—in field work, domestic tasks, child rearing, and food gathering and preparation. In quite a few cultures polygyny may be *the preferred* custom, but not all men can afford to maintain two or more wives—the economic feature of marriage. In some cultures, the multiple wives live in the same household with separate quarters; in others a man must provide separate residences. I recall one of my students from the Middle East reporting to the class that she was studying in the United States because her father (who had two wives) had provided an American university education to the children of his first wife and was required to do the same for the children of his second wife (this student's mother). She further expanded on this economic issue by noting that whatever was provided for wife #1 and her offspring must be provided for wife #2 and her children. In her family each wife had a house of equal value and received gifts from her husband that were the same or of equal value. Details such as this regarding the economic aspect of marriage differ widely and are interesting to explore.

Before my first anthropology class, I was unaware of cultures where women had more than one husband. There are not many of these (three cultures out of 400 in Robert Textor's [1967] report), but the fact of their existence led me to wanting to know why. The study of kinship across cultures was one of the aspects of the discipline that drew me in and caused me to switch my major to anthropology.

In cultures that practice *polyandry* (a woman with more than one husband), like those that practice polygyny, the custom can often be explained by examining economic issues. For example, when brothers share a wife, large male-owned land holdings need not be divided when property is passed to the next generation. Thus, a woman married to brothers is the common practice in polyandrous societies such as Tibetans living in northern Nepal. In the past, monogamy was primarily found in small foraging/hunting/gathering societies, and in more recent historical times, it is practiced in a variety of societies. Monogamy is the most common marriage form today. Yet, polygyny, as noted above, is still the most *preferred ideal* among world cultures. In a 1967 survey based on the Human Relations Area Files data, only 81 cultures out of a sample of 400 cultures preferred monogamy, though economic realities kept men from having more than one wife (Textor 1967:124). Note that there have been hypotheses other than the economic one to explain the popularity of polygyny, and it may be that there were different reasons such a custom evolved in each culture. As in other essays in this book, however, I like a straightforward functionalist explanation for the existence of customs, and economics makes sense to me.

Same-sex marriage is also reported in the anthropological literature. Such unions have been recognized in cultures in Africa, Asia, the Pacific, pre-Columbian Native American cultures, and those of historic Greece and Rome (Eskridge 1993: 25). There is also a report of recognized group marriage during historic times where the Kaingang of Brazil had 8 percent of the population practicing group marriage. In North American hippie communes of the 1960s it was often declared that every adult member was married to everyone else. In this case, however, such "unions" were not legally sanctioned by the state or recognized by most members of North American culture.

Definitions of marriage are social constructs that may change over time. A social construct is a meaning that a group of people create and agree on. This seems to be what is happening in the United States today as around half of the population accepts same-sex marriage, and the laws of several states currently allow same-sex couples to marry, thus recognizing this as a legal union. The recent Supreme Court ruling over the California initiative furthers this change process and paves the way for legal recognition of same-sex couples in other states.

I believe that an important achievement of anthropology is that it makes one aware of the differences and similarities among peoples of the world. Less awareness leaves one open to *ethnocentrism*. Ethnocentrism creates problems personally and politically and interferes with a host of issues, both domestic and international. I am not suggesting that people who study other cultures will change, or should change, their minds as to how they think about marriage or other customs and values, but I believe it will make them more accepting of others' beliefs and customs.

I'll be thinking about all of this when I attend the wedding ceremony this afternoon. You might do the same the next time you attend a wedding ceremony.

Update 2019: On June 26, 2015, the United States Supreme Court ruled that same-sex couples can marry nationwide. The 5–4 ruling held that states cannot ban same-sex marriage. As of 2018 25 countries have officially legalized same-sex marriage nationwide. In a few additional countries same-sex marriage is legal only for some regions of the country; in other nations same-sex unions are still against the law.

Challenge: From the perspective of your subculture what are the features of marriage?

Thinking It Through

• Delineate the common features of marriage found cross-culturally.
• Identify how and why the term "marriage" is, in fact, a social construct.

Anthropological Terms

enculturated   polygyny
ethnocentrism   social construct
polyandry

Thinking Practically

• What part does economics play in a decision to marry in Western cultures today?
• In what way does ethnocentrism cause problems when considering a definition of marriage?
• Does the preceding discussion lead you to alter your views about the definition of marriage?

14 ~ Zip Your Lip

Advice columnists are repeatedly asked to help solve issues relating to how to deal with in-laws. This essay places the issue within the perspective of cross-cultural kinship systems.

"Bite your tongue." "Zip your lip." "Learn what triggers conflict." "Avoid them." From advice columns to wikiHow and other websites these are the most mentioned strategies to deal with your *in-laws*. Questions about how to handle relationships with in-laws appear often in the "Ask Amy" advice column of my local paper (a column picked up from the *Chicago Tribune*)—"My (fill in the blank)-in-law is: causing family problems, causing me or my spouse stress, driving me crazy, ruining my life." It is not just mothers-in-law, the butt of many jokes by comedians, who cause conflict, although they top the list of in-law issues—mostly husbands' mothers. Queries are also made to Amy and other advice columnists about problems with daughters-in-law, sons-in-law, fathers-in-law, sisters- and brothers-in–law, and even more distant in-laws.

Dilemmas involving in-laws contribute to feelings of anxiety, anger, and frustration for letter writers. These people want advice and quick solutions from an objective "expert." Common in-law "issues" range from planning a wedding, gift giving, child rearing and discipline, pet behavior, and spousal behaviors, to how money is spent, loaned, and repaid (or not). Major themes in these letters are lack of mutual respect, or appreciation, and poor communication. Extrapolating from the number of in-law-related letters I read in the "Ask Amy" column, it is clear that many, many families are plagued by such concerns. When I read one of these letters, I think about my own experiences with my mother- and father-in-law—they span nearly 30 years of my marriage and have evoked all the feelings and several of the issues and themes expressed by the letter writers. I often wish that our culture, like many others I've studied, had a strong rule of mother-in-law avoidance.

In-law issues are not unique to North American culture. In-law relationships cause many of the above listed feelings in all cultures. These issues are considered private matters in many cultures and are not discussed openly as they tend to be here—a cultural difference often noted by foreign visitors to North America. Anthropology's ethnographic literature, however, provides resources for the comparison and contrast of cultural ideals and realities associated with family and in-laws.

In contemporary Western societies there is no universally practiced kinship system to provide guidance for our behavior toward kin, particularly outside the nuclear family. This lack of an overarching kinship system that directs, regulates, and controls our behaviors results in us riding, in effect, in a ship without a rudder. We are products of what I'll call our "free choice" system of kinship; as such we often do not know what reciprocal behaviors and responsibilities we have toward relatives, and we get tossed in waves of uncertainty, frustration, and anger. Hence the many cries for help from advice columnists, as we hope they will know how to once again bring peace to the family. The advice given often makes sense, but the advisors are essentially making it up as they go along because there is no cultural book of rules today for most North American and European kin relationships. Recent immigrants from cultures that practice detailed kinship systems often maintain these for a couple of generations if they reside in ethnic enclaves. Such enclaves continually reinforce old traditions, including those that direct and control the behaviors of their members toward kin.

Learning one's culture is a long and difficult process. Much of what constitutes one's culture is not taught in a classroom, or by family. This is what anthropologist Edward T. Hall, in his seminal book *The Silent Language* (1973), calls the hidden dimension of culture. We learn about it mostly by experiencing, watching, and listening. Kin relations are one such hidden domain.

Every human belongs to a *family of orientation*, the family that one is born into. And most people will also become part of a *family of procreation* during their lifetime—the nuclear family that they establish when they marry. In-laws are the extended kin one acquires on marriage—these are called *affinal kin*. The focus in North American traditional culture is what we call the *nuclear family of orientation*. It consists of our biological mother and father plus siblings born to these two people. In anthropology-speak these blood relatives are called our *consanguineal kin*. But wait, what about children who are adopted, born of surrogates, and donated eggs and sperm? That such issues occur to you reflect the scientific facts that you take for granted today. A *nuclear family* is defined in anthropological kinship research as a family with two married adults and their *legally recognized* offspring. So if a person's biological parents are not married, is this still considered a nuclear family? And, what if your mother was married (or not) to your biological father and then was divorced and remarried—which family unit is your nuclear family? More on this issue momentarily. Meanwhile back to the nuclear family of orientation.

Our nuclear family of orientation is where each of us is schooled in how to relate to all of our kin—both consanguineal (blood relatives) and affinal (relatives by marriage, such as your father's brother's wife, or your husband's mother). This is enculturation at work. Much of what we learn is done by observing how mother relates to father, brother relates to sister, mother relates to daughter, daughter relates to mother and father, father relates to son, son relates to mother, son relates to father and mother. We listen to playmates and school friends when they talk about the members of their family. Sometimes a parent will tell us how to behave toward one of these individuals—at least our cultural ideal of how to behave: for example, "love and respect your father." As we grow, we experience con-

107

tacts with members of our extended family as well and again learn about expected role behaviors mostly by observation. Extended family includes aunts, uncles, cousins, grandparents, and second cousins. Blood relationships are pointed out to us—Uncle Jim is dad's brother; Aunt Sally is married to Uncle Jim so she is not a blood relative; Cousin Robert is a blood relative because he is Uncle Jim's son. We gradually build an inventory of these relationships. And, as many know, this inventory becomes quite complex with divorce or death and remarriage plus acquiring half-siblings and step-siblings.

A person's kin group consists of consanguineal relatives and affinal relatives. A *kinship system* refers to the *culturally constructed* complex system of rules developed by a culture that govern consanguineal and affinal kin. In most cultures relatives treated as consanguines include individuals who are adopted, individuals conceived from donated sperm, and individuals born of surrogate mothers. In many cultures a child raised by a couple is considered their blood kin with or without a formal legal adoption. In past times the actual biological relation of a child's father or mother was not a reason for concern; today, with easy access to DNA tests, paternity and maternity is an issue for many. Still, from a kinship system perspective, all of these individuals belong to the category consanguineal kin. The many recent technological and scientific findings about reproduction were not issues when our ancestors developed kinship systems. The known kinship systems were in place before the time of written records; their origins are unknown. We hypothesize that smart leaders dictated these systems, because having rules in place made for less conflict and defined issues such as who is economically responsible for a child.

We have recorded detailed kinship systems from hundreds of cultures. The most detailed and well-defined kinship systems are found in tribal societies and are still practiced by many of them. In these systems individuals are enculturated to know who they are, how to behave toward specific kin, and what to expect from them. From an outsider's view (the *etic* view) such a system may seem stifling and rigid (an ethnocentric reaction); from the view of a person within one of these cultures (an *emic* view) the system provides security and comfort when dealing with interpersonal relationships because roles and their associated behaviors are spelled out. This is not to say that the insider is always happy doing what is expected by her or his culture. Ethnographic research on kinship contains not just descriptions of what ideal system is practiced but also reports of variations and deviations that occur and how they are addressed.

When kinship data are compared, they fall into categories based on how *descent* is traced, either through males (termed *patrilineal systems*), through females (termed *matrilineal systems*), or both male and female (termed *bilateral or kindred systems*). Within these descent system structures are *terminological systems. Kinship terms* are words that designate relationships between consanguines and affines; these terms are *cultural constructs* that specify social relationships and focus primarily on an individual's own generation and that of his or her parents.

Kinship systems function to organize people into groups (family, lineage, clan). Within these groups behaviors are assigned to individuals and behaviors are regulated and in many cases controlled. For example, "mother" is defined as a biological female parent. She should be protective, nurturing, and loving while she teaches her children about their culture and how to survive in it. Reciprocally, her children have expected behaviors toward her—love, respect, and help when needed. For each kinship term there are reciprocal roles and expectations. Continue to keep in mind that anthropologists focus on describing ideal roles and behaviors that are dictated by a kinship system.

Several terminological patterns are repeated in world cultures, and although the languages differ, the patterns of usage are the same. The so-called Eskimo system pattern is the one used in traditional North American and European cultures. It focuses on the nuclear family. There is one word for mother and one word for father; siblings are called brother or sister. In one's parents' generation, the parents' siblings are all lumped together as aunt or uncle (in this system the same term is used for both consanguineal and affinal aunts and uncles). Cousins are lumped, too, by a single term; that is, no clue as to the sex of these persons is found in the term. The statement, "My cousin visited yesterday," doesn't give us much information in this terminological system: Is this a cousin on your mother's side or your father's side and is the cousin male or female? When we use the term aunt we have generally been enculturated to respect this person who is a relative, but beyond that, the Eskimo system does not give us much guidance as to how we should treat our aunts or how they should behave toward us.

In contrast to the Eskimo system are other systems of terminology that carry very specific dictates about behaviors toward not only members of one's nuclear family but toward, for example, cousins. To illustrate: In the Iroquois system there are individual kin terms for various cousin categories—your mother's sister's children are called by terms that reflect their sex and that they are your mother's sister's kids. Your mother's brother's children are called by different terms. So if you are a male member of the Yąnomamö tribe, where terminology follows the Iroquois system, and you tell a friend that your *suaboya* visited, your friend will know that you had a visit from your father's sister's daughter or your mother's brother's daughter. If you are a female, you call your father's sister's son and your mother's brother's son "*soriwa*." Along with knowing this information conveyed by the term you use (either *suaboya* or *soriwa*), your friend will also know that this person is a cousin, is in the category of female or male, and is your ideal marriage partner. Cousin marriage, while not commonly practiced in North American culture, is practiced in many world cultures. The point here is that there are kinship systems that consist of kin terminology that directs, regulates, and controls the behaviors of people. And, this forestalls many of the in-law and other issues of family relations that plague us in the Eskimo terminological system where roles are not well defined. Anthropologists have identified six terminological systems that are common. Most other terminological systems are variations on each of these. For more information on terminological systems check out this excellent website on kinship that includes diagrams and discussion of the six common systems: https://umanitoba.ca/faculties/arts/anthropology/tutor/kinterms/termsys.html

When I taught at a Canadian college I often had students from various Native Canadian tribes in my classes. When we were on the topic of kinship they often shared their culture's kinship system, kinship terminology, and customs associated with the treatment of consanguineal and affinal relatives. One male student shared with the class his tribe's solution to the mother-in-law issue—avoidance. If he was in the bedroom when she came to visit his wife, he either stayed behind the closed door or exited through the bedroom window! An objective perspective on this custom would, I believe, view it as very functional in avoiding conflict. Certainly my student strongly voiced this view. Avoidance also functions as a show of respect—by avoiding the relative with whom numerous conflicts might arise, you show her respect.

In a major study of world kinship reported by George Peter Murdock in his 1949 book *Social Structure* he included data on mother-in-law avoidance taboos. Of 250 societies, 137 were reported to have avoidance taboos. These ranged from informal avoidance of a man's wife's mother (i.e., he stays away from situations where he might encounter her) (26 cultures), respect or reserved behavior when in her presence (33 cultures), and true avoidance (78 cultures) (Murdock: 1949: 277). True avoidance meant that a man must leave the area if he sees his wife's mother coming.

Knowing how other cultures treat affinal kin gives us a broader and deeper understanding of the human experience. And, it forces us to reflect on the adaptive flexibility of this core cultural domain. A major reason to study the data of anthropology is that by studying and contemplating other cultures, we learn more about our own. Perhaps the advice given by Amy to "bite your tongue" or "avoid" troublesome in-laws or situations that trigger conflict with them is grounded in the mists of time when our ancient ancestors realized that by making such strategies part of the structure of kinship they reduced stress and conflict.

Challenge: How do you think North American life would change if we practiced mother-in-law avoidance in our culture?

Thinking It Through
- Identify types of descent groups found across cultures.
- Explain the mother-in-law taboo across cultures.
- Explain the importance of in-laws within kinship systems.

Anthropological Terms

affinal kin	kinship system
bilateral or kindred system	kinship term
consanguineal kin	matrilineal system
emic	nuclear family
etic	nuclear family of orientation
family of orientation	patrilineal system
family of procreation	terminological system
in-law	

Thinking Practically
- Do you talk openly with friends about stressful issues that you have with your kin? If you are married and have in-laws, how do your relationships with them differ from your relationships with your consanguines?
- Do you agree with the old saying, "Blood is thicker than water"? Why or why not? How does this old saying underscore the fact that kinship systems are cultural constructs?
- Describe how "in-law" conflicts are used in contemporary television sitcoms. Cite a specific example.

15 ~ Unforeseen Consequences

A plumbing emergency due to an unforeseen consequence of a change in federal water use standards required an expensive fix to the author's home. This essay reviews some of the history of how culture changes and how impact studies and applied anthropology may aid planners to anticipate unforeseen consequences of change.

I suddenly felt the shower water covering my feet. Huh? In record time I rinsed the soap and shampoo lather from my body and hair and turned the water off. The shower floor was not draining at all. Yikes. This was Easter morning and family was due for brunch and egg hunts soon. Wrapping in a towel I tried to flush the toilet. Nothing.

A call to Rescue Rooter, after we had tried but failed to get things moving with our emergency plunger, resulted in a temporary fix that got us through the day. We ultimately needed an expensive sewer line replacement. Our contractor put the issue into perspective when he said this was happening all over northern California in older neighborhoods—an unforeseen consequence of technological change over time. In this case, the new technology was low water usage appliances. No one foresaw their incompatibility with older domestic sewage systems.

Due to the persistent five-year California drought, we had installed low water usage toilets, further cut down on water use by not flushing every #1 use of the toilet (a strategy encouraged by the local water districts), and purchased a low water use washing machine. These efforts to be good citizens and reduce water usage took their toll. Neither we nor the advocates of reduction in domestic water use—water companies and governmental water agencies—foresaw possible consequences of people's efforts to conserve water. Our neighborhood's 50-year-old sewer pipe system was designed to utilize several gallons per flush, thus moving waste out from our property to the large sewer pipes beneath the street. Older toilets use between 3.5, 6, or even 7 gallons per flush (GPF), while new federal plumbing standards dictate 1.6 GPF and some new high efficiency toilets use a piddling 1.28 GPF. The old higher-volume per flush was keeping our sewer contents moving.

My husband and I began to discuss the process of culture change. We reviewed the history of change in anthropological research plus all of the tales of unforeseen consequences of planned change that we had studied. I also began in earnest to be on the alert for contemporary examples.

Culture change is initiated through both *innovations* (totally new and unique technologies and ideas), and *inventions* (creations based on new combinations of materials and techniques already in existence). The wheel was an innovation; notching wheels to create gears was an invention as were myriad other inventions based on the idea of the wheel. In the early 1900s, as data about world cultures increased, anthropologists developed hypotheses about how cultural elements spread from one geographic region to another and gathered data about the often unforeseen consequences of this culture change. One early 1900s' theoretical school of thought was called the *Diffusionist School*; it attempted to collect evidence for the *diffusion* (borrowing) of objects and ideas between cultures around the world as they came into contact. Borrowing, it was reasoned, was easier for people than innovation or invention, hence more common and rapid. A subgroup of theorists known as the *Heliocentric Diffusionists* argued that many innovations and inventions began in ancient Egypt and diffused from there in concentric circles to the far reaches of the planet—from designs on pottery to types of watercraft and tools. It was soon realized that both of these early hypotheses were simplistic, and the study of change processes intensified.

During the early 1950s anthropologist George Foster and colleagues were Smithsonian Institution teaching and research social scientists working in Latin America. They analyzed the role of social and cultural factors affecting the work and outcome of public health center programs. Foster's interests coalesced as he researched, directed, and collaborated in culture change programs around the world—projects in, for example, public health, community development, engineering, and education. He developed theories about culture change and outlined barriers—social, psychological, and cultural—that led to *unforeseen consequences* in planned change programs. He also developed a list of the most effective stimulants for change. These include desire for economic gain and competitive situations. His seminal work *Traditional Cultures: and the Impact of Technological Change* (Foster 1962) is considered a foundation of what is today's **applied anthropology.**

Culture change is complex; cultures are not static, change is constant, and parts of cultures change at different rates. You will recall from an earlier essay that culture is learned and its parts are integrated. Value systems differ from culture to culture and can have an impact on any change, *how* it occurs, *if* it occurs, and—if it is a planned program of change—whether it happens according to the plan. Information on culture change resulting from ethnographic restudies and postproject **impact studies** accumulated through the decades since Foster's initial work. Impact studies use ethnographic methods to look at a situation and its context during and/or after a program is implemented. Today, the subdiscipline of applied anthropology draws on all we've learned about culture change and applies it to assessing proposed projects with a goal of identifying and ameliorating potential unforeseen consequences. Following are classic and contemporary examples.

Corn and Custom

The case of the introduction of hybrid corn to farmers in New Mexico is a classic case study of how human cultural elements can cause unforeseen difficulties in the success of programs of planned change. This was a community of Spanish American farmers who grew a native variety of corn, known as Indian corn. The farmers saved seed each year from the harvest for planting the next year's crop. The corn yielded 25 bushels per acre. There was sufficient water from the nearby river for irrigation and soil fertility was maintained by the addition of some manure each year. The corn was used primarily to make tortillas, a diet staple for the people. A local mill ground the corn at this time, though in the past grinding was done by hand using a *mano* (handheld grinding stone) on a stone mortar called a *metate*.

A United States Department of Agriculture farmer extension advisor had worked in the area for several years. He spoke Spanish, had good rapport with the farmers, and was familiar with their farming practices. At a community meeting he proposed to the villagers that they try growing a hybrid variety of corn that would yield about 100 bushels per acre; it was also disease resistant. The advisor discussed this high yield hybrid corn with community leaders and showed a movie about it. Finally, a demonstration plot of the hybrid corn was grown near the village so farmers could judge its advantage for themselves. The next season 40 farmers out of 84 grew plots of the hybrid. The following season 60 farmers grew the hybrid. Harvest yields were high, double that of the Indian corn. Then hybrid planting dropped: first to only 30 farmers, then only three, and there had been no diffusion of the hybrid corn to surrounding villages. Virtually everyone else was back to planting the Indian corn. No one reported any difficulties in obtaining the hybrid seed, they acknowledged the vigor of the hybrid, and all said they were pleased with the higher yields (Apodaca 1952: 35–39). What happened?

From the first harvest the farmers' wives complained about the new corn. The hybrid corn did not have the proper texture they said, and it made poor tortillas that fell apart easily; they also felt that the tortillas did not taste right, and they disliked the color of the tortillas the corn produced. Some farmers still planted the hybrid for a couple of seasons and used it as animal feed. But the unhappy wives, in the end, persuaded the farmers to return to the traditional Indian corn. Cultural values and traditional attitudes had acted as barriers to change even though the extension agent had used good *technical* practices in his program of planned change. Values and tradition were identified retrospectively as cultural barriers to change in many projects worldwide. The lesson to take from this study is that careful technological planning alone may not be enough to avoid failure of a project.

Plastics

In the 1967 film *The Graduate*, Benjamin is celebrating his university graduation at a family party, and Mr. McGuire, a family friend, is offering advice that he thinks will secure Ben's future:

MR. MCGUIRE: "I want to say one word to you. Just one word."
BENJAMIN: "Yes, sir."
MR. MCGUIRE: "Are you listening?"
BENJAMIN: "Yes, I am."
MR. MCGUIRE: "Plastics!" (Ehlers 2007)

This dialogue (number 42 in the top 100 cinematic quotes of all time) is immediately recognized today by generations of Stanford University graduates and others across the country. Part of the celebration of *their* rite of passage is a campus screening of the film where they laugh and cheer through this retro, yet ever timely and poignant, film. Little did any of us who saw the film the year it was originally released give a thought to the unforeseen consequences of the development of plastics. Indeed, this is not an example of a planned change program per se; rather it is an example of a technological innovation—undertaken to make money and provide new consumer products—that has had unforeseen consequences over time.

Consumer plastic products began appearing after World War II when the manufacturing plants built to construct war equipment, from radar insulations to vehicles, sought other uses for petrochemical-based plastics;

Tupperware, for example, was first available in 1948, and the material quickly began to be used for purposes other than storage containers. Plastics in the most commonly used form are not biodegradable. They are rapidly turning landfills and Earth's oceans into junkyards of plastic debris small and large, a dire unforeseen consequence of consumers' enthusiasm for items made of this material. Tons of the stuff pour into the oceans through drains and waterways. In 1975, the National Academy of Sciences gave a rough estimate of 0.1 percent for the amount of annual global plastic production ending up in the world's oceans. A study conducted in 2010 revised this estimate; it reported the amount to be 1.5 percent to 4.5 percent, meaning that 4 million to 12 million metric tons of plastic was swept into our oceans that year from 192 world coastal countries that have significant coastal populations (Chen 2015). Small organisms ingest plastic particles and die or are eaten by larger organisms such as fish that in turn are eaten by marine mammals whose systems become compromised and they die. Plastic debris is everywhere, and it is choking the planet and its inhabitants.

Mosquito Nets

And as a final contemporary example: the unforeseen consequence of the distribution of mosquito netting by well-meaning charity organizations. The use of insecticide-treated mosquito netting in regions of the world plagued by malaria-bearing mosquitos is saving lives. This technology works and is relatively inexpensive. Many charitable organizations began campaigns to distribute these nets. The unforeseen consequence of this act has been surfacing for some time. Poor and starving people need more than protection from mosquitos. Zambia, for example, was the recipient of many donations of mosquito nets, over nine million of which were distributed in 2013 and 2014 by the Zambian government working with the United Nations and various donors. People welcomed them. Cases of malaria dropped significantly. Then another problem began to surface (Bowers 2014; Gentleman 2015). Impact studies gathered data showing an alarming decrease in the availability of dietary protein in this and other areas—fisheries were in decline. It turns out that over much of the world where free mosquito nets were being distributed, they were often sewn together and used as nets for fishing. Net fishing with these nets of very tiny holes resulted in the devastation of lakes, streams, rivers, and shores as fishermen raked in everything—shellfish, fish eggs fingerlings, larger fish—leaving barren environments. The fisheries did not naturally restock as when the old handmade nets with large holes were used. Additionally, the insecticides in the nets were being washed into water. Currently local governments are passing laws against using the nets for fishing (Baragone 2018). In nutrient poor areas this may not stop the use of nets for fishing. This case illustrates why a holistic and careful approach to culture change should be part of the equation. A prestudy that included participant-observation in the target cultures could have structured the charitable work in a manner that ameliorated this unforeseen consequence.

Change happens, some through planned projects and some through the processes of innovation, invention, and diffusion. A consideration of traditional cultural values and situational context may improve the success of planned programs and help to forestall unforeseen consequences. Project prestudies based on anthropology's field methods, in particular *participant-observation*, can provide context for planning change. Our perspectives and methods are now recognized by many in the business sector and in governmental agencies, and they are hiring anthropologists as part of their teams.

Today I placed an Amazon order. When I hit the place order button and sat back, pleased with my purchase, I suddenly began to contemplate what unforeseen consequences may occur in the future as more and more of us do more and more of our shopping online. Like the low water use toilet and washing machine, will online shopping ultimately cost me? And how could an anthropological approach to studying this phenomenon help to avoid a major unforeseen consequence?

Challenge: Make a list of possible unforeseen consequences of the massive replacement of fossil fuel cars (and trucks) by electric vehicles (EVs).

Thinking It Through

- What ethnographic method developed by anthropologists might have foreseen the barriers to adoption of the hybrid corn in New Mexico? How might the barriers that doomed the project have been overcome?
- Hypothesize why values and traditions are frequently overlooked when technological change is being developed.
- Discuss the potential unforeseen consequences of the increased popularity of commercial solar installations nationwide.

Anthropological Terms

applied anthropology	invention
diffusion	mano
impact study	metate
innovation	participant-observation

Thinking Practically

- Identify and discuss two unforeseen consequences of the use of digital college textbooks in lieu of hard copies.
- Identify and discuss two unforeseen consequences of the use of household pesticides.

16 ~ Dogs and Cats

*The role of pets in everyday human life is examined against
the backdrop of culture—how we value and treat them,
what past history reveals, and the benefits of pets to individuals and to society today.*

My neighbor Judy is walking her dog Kisha, a Shih Tzu. I often join
them for the exercise and social time. First from around the corner comes
Tim who is walking PoPo, a basset hound mix. Larry approaches from
the other direction walking Maddy, a small terrier mix. We all briefly stop
and greet; the dogs by sniffing each other and tail wagging, we humans
smile and chitchat about current events. Continuing our neighborhood
circuit we meet my friend Bev walking her dogs Scuba, a terrier mix, and
Skylar, a Golden Lab. These dogs are friends of Kisha, too, and we again
stop to chat while the dogs interact. Over our 45-minute walk we bump
into four other neighbors out dog walking. All of them carry little plastic
doggie-doo bags that they use periodically to pick up after their pet; it is
part of the dog walking code.

I've often thought, while participating in the walking ritual, that this
and other aspects of North American *cultural values* and behaviors might
seem odd and elicit *ethnocentric* reactions from people of other world
cultures. I consider my field experiences on several islands in Polynesia
(Tahiti, Tahaa, Moorea, Huahini, Bora Bora, Rarotonga, and Aitutaki)
where dogs wandered about at will (often termed "wandering dogs"). No

one walked them or paid them much attention. In the Spanish village I lived in for several months I only saw a dog on a leash being walked one time and none of the families I knew had a pet.

I've also considered what pets provide for both individuals and society. One function of pet ownership seen from my anthropological perspective is pets provide an integrative mechanism. Anthropologist Elman Service used the term *sodality* to describe this form of integration as human societies progressed from *bands* to *tribes* to *states*. The term, in my opinion, applies to many interest or hobby groups today. A sodality is a group with no kin or residence basis that crosscuts a society and acts as an integrative agent. Here is background to my assertion: Tribal societies, as defined by anthropologists, do not have centralized leadership or authority with any form of coercive power (the use of force). Tribes often consist of thousands of people. They are kin based. Kin groups and complex marriage relationships are the threads that weave the society together; another thread is the sodality. Ethnologists like Elman Service noted a common custom that connected people in large tribes—*age-sets*. Young men were initiated into manhood across the entire tribal culture at regular intervals and thus became affiliated with men from distant places. These age-sets were termed *pantribal sodalities*. Each age-set initiate group was given a name, shared the initiation experience, and became comrades for life. Sometimes they acted together in conflicts with other tribes when involved in warfare. Ethnographers note that when two strangers met on an African veldt, for example, they would greet each other by asking the identity of each other's tribe, clan, or lineage. If no common relationship was found they would then ask about age-set affiliation. Even the age-set of one's older brother or cousin would suffice to label one a friend rather than an enemy. Women were typically known as being part of the age-set affiliation of their husband.

What threads bind the fabric of twenty-first century urban-centered state societies? Kinship certainly creates ties with others, even for those who live in cities and towns hundreds or thousands of miles apart. Common work, religion, or politics also serves to give us a sense of community with others, but these are based on institutions within our society. Most interest groups are not tied to formal segments of a society. From an anthropological perspective, sodalities today are the sources of myriad threads that are spun across our geographical and social fabric. These interest groups hold us together in important ways, as they crosscut ethnic, religious, gender, socioeconomic, and political boundaries. I believe it is appropriate to borrow the term sodality when addressing the functions of pet associations such as the American Kennel Club, the American Cat Fanciers Association, The Goldfish Council, or the American Fancy Rat & Mouse Association since they fit the basics of the definition of a sodality. I assert that most *informal* interest groups in large societies function as integrative mechanisms, too—from gamers to gardeners, from surfers to skaters, from coin collectors to classic car collectors. The list of such groups is extensive, and I believe having a family pet functions this way as well. Without these sodality mechanisms large modern societies would be much more fragmented; our world would be more fragmented, too. I have noted that people surrounded by strangers—e.g., on a bus or a plane; in a youth hostel, dormitory, new class, or B&B; or at a cocktail party—often strive in their initial conversations to establish some connection. Identifying a connection makes one, if not a friend, at least not a complete stranger. The next time you experience being in such a situation wear your anthropological lens and note when connections are made. How often does finding out you both have a similar hobby, dog, cat, or other pet provide this?

Once primarily appraised for their qualities of assisting humans—in tasks such as hunting, security and warning of approaching enemies, rodent control, and protection of grain storage facilities—dogs, cats, and other animals are now often viewed as a part of one's family, rather like children. They are played with, fed, and given comfy beds, other special furniture, and toys. We can subscribe for monthly deliveries of surprise boxes of new toys and treats from businesses like Bark Box for dogs and Meow Box for cats. We take them to vets for wellness checkups and to receive vaccinations. We have them groomed—baths, nail trims, haircuts.

After neutering a male dog (technically a dog is a male; a bitch a female) owners concerned for the dog's appearance (and perhaps, as the ads say, the dog's own self-image) can provide the creature a more natural look by having the veterinarian implant a set of Neuticles, testicular implants.

Recently while at a popular seaside park along the central California coast we watched with some amusement when an SUV pulled in to the parking area and the driver opened the back hatch and nine dogs spilled out. They were big and small, and of various breeds. The driver grabbed several balls and chased after the dogs, throwing the balls and calling the dogs by name. This was clearly familiar routine as the animals responded by returning the balls and romping about barking until he threw the balls again. We briefly spoke to the driver when he took a break. He told us this was his dog-sitting and -walking business. He picks the dogs up and returns them to their homes after several hours of exercise and social time. On demand dog-walking services, such as "Wag" and "Rover," are increasing in popularity. Just like Uber, they have apps for easy booking and payment.

Camp Bow Wow, a dog care and boarding facility with franchises all over my state of California as well as across the nation, is an example of our cultural value to focus on the well-being of our pets in much the same way we care for our children, by signing them up for camp activities during school breaks. A Camp Bow Wow is located near my home. It is not representative of the boarding kennels of the past. At Camp Bow Wow, dogs are treated to an active day with exercise, socialization with other dogs and people, and mental stimulation. The facility includes climate controlled indoor play yards and outdoor play yards. There are camp counselors who have CPR and first aid training as well as training in dog behavior. Should you need to leave your dog overnight he or she will have a private cabin with a fleece padded cot and special evening treats. Owners can check on their pets from their phones and computers through a live web cam. The website tells us that one's dog is relieved of the boredom and destructive behavior that may manifest in a dog left home alone all day.

Offering dog owners' opportunities to socialize is another function of dog ownership in today's culture. Dedicated dog hotels abound. One can leave a dog at the hotel for the day and after work join other dog parents for play with the dogs in the outdoor dog park, enjoy a coffee, and socially interact. Dog parks—fenced areas with water spigots and bowls, shade structures, and often obstacle courses—have been built recently in my small city. I observed one such new dog park last week. It was filled with dogs romping with owners and other dogs and owners interacting. Dog parks are alternatives to meeting and socializing in bars or clubs.

For cat people there are opportunities to socialize while interacting with felines in cat cafés, tearooms, and bars. Taipei, Taiwan, is generally credited with starting the cat tearoom craze, which quickly spread to Japan and beyond. Both cat tearooms and cat bars (these serve alcoholic beverages) are now popular the world over—France, England, Spain, Canada, Germany, Hungary, India, Thailand, Russia, and the United States. These and other countries boast cat tearooms in major cities and promote them as special places for both locals and tourists to stop for refreshment. Customers pay a fee to enjoy time with felines—watching their antics, petting them, perhaps having a lap companion—while sipping tea or other beverages and munching treats like the paw print cookies on the menu at KitTea Cat Café in San Francisco, California. In Montreal, Canada, Le Café des Chats boasts an on-site veterinarian available for consultation. These establishments are particularly popular in densely populated cities such as Osaka, Japan, where there are often mandated no-pet policies in apartment buildings. Some of the cat cafés are associated with cat sanctuaries or rescue groups, and the kitties roaming the café can be adopted.

The number of pets in the United States—dogs, cats, fish, rabbits, ferrets, hamsters, pigs, reptiles, birds, and others—is huge. There are 89.7 million pet dogs and 92.4 million pet cats (Statista 2017/2018). How did we come to value pets and consider them as part of our family? *Enculturation* that begins in the home is part of the answer. My own history with pets includes a dog, hamsters, parakeets, a rat, tropical fish, chickens, and cats. The chickens—Lady, Bug, Snow, and White; Lemon, Meringue, and Pie; Big Red, Henny Penny, and the Hot Cross Buns—provided 35 years of entertainment, plus fresh eggs. Prince Ah Pooh, my first cat, gave me companionship and hours of fun when I was a child; Smudge the cat was adopted during my first weeks of marriage and was a treasured member of our family for 19 years. More recently, Mr. Darwin and Mrs. Hobbes came to live with us when our daughter left for college; they brought laughter with their antics, gave us purrs, warmed our laps, and inspired my writing.

In addition to learning to value pets through our family's attitudes toward them, media contributes to the process. Cats and dogs are in the comics and on television sitcoms, the internet, YouTube, Facebook, and Snapchat posts. Have you watched any cat videos on YouTube? Dogs and cats act as companions, confidants, and foils for children and adults. From Lassie of early television and movies, to Snoopy of the comics and beyond, children and dogs are visibly linked. Currently, Rover the charming companion to Red in the comic strip *Red and Rover* by Brian Basset (2009) is my favorite; it often prods philosophical thoughts. Dogs are in many other of today's comic strips too: Earl in *Mutts*, Puddles in *Luann*, and Roscoe in *Pickles*. Cats are also in the comics—the popular lasagna-eating cat Garfield in *Garfield*, Muffin in *Pickles*, and Mooch in *Mutts*, among others.

Paleontologists and archaeologists tell us that dogs were first domesticated between 10,000 and 32,000 years ago. The analysis of fossil finds and ancient DNA studies are still sorting the details of when and where their DNA began to differ from wolves. Cats became domesticated between 10,000 and 15,000 years ago. Both animals have practical functions that our ancestors likely recognized, certainly by the time people were living in settlements and growing food crops. Dogs can be trained by hunters to assist in tracking, flushing, and retrieving prey; dogs can clean up scraps of food; dogs can sound the alarm of an intruder by barking. Cats aid in the control of vermin, including rats and mice who eat stored grains and who carry diseases.

Humans treating dogs and cats as family seems normal to those of us living today, particularly in Western societies. The historical and ethnographic data on the subject of dogs and cats as pets, however, are limited. I suspect this is simply an error of omission. Ethnographies seldom referenced pets. When included, dogs are reported as being useful for hunting, warning of the approach of enemies, or for transportation, as with the Inuit who use them for pulling sleds across the frozen tundra. A monkey or small piglet is sometimes mentioned as being carried about or played with by an individual, but ethnographers focused on describing economics, technology, kinship, and politics, and still do. Early historical records scribed on clay tablets or parchments also mostly focused on issues such as economics, politics, and religion. Pictographic representations from early times do show the occasional cat or dog, but their place relative to individual humans is unclear.

The exception is the place of cats in ancient Egypt. A cat deity was worshiped; it is depicted in murals and sculptures as half cat (the head) and half woman (from the neck down). Cat mummies found in Egyptian tombs are thought to have been placed there to accompany the Pharaohs to the next life along with members of the Pharaoh's household and other animals. Thousands of remains of cats have been excavated from burial tombs and pyramids; one large tomb contained 80,000 cat mummies. Visit the British Museum in London, as I have, to see some good examples. It is still unclear the part cats played in an individual's everyday life aside from the very real service of cats in the elimination of rodent vermin. Were they pets in the sense we use the term today? John Bradshaw, an *anthrozoologist* (the science of human and animal interactions), reports that nobles and royals during the Middle Ages kept pets such as dogs, cats, and birds and treated them well; he suggests caring for pets is an instinctual human behavior (Bradshaw 2017). We also know that cats were widely feared during the Middle Ages when they were thought by many to be witches. During the European Renaissance, cats appeared in literature and paintings. One portrait by the Italian Renaissance painter Francesco d'Ubertino Verdi shows a seated woman caressing a cat in her lap.

Anthrozoology draws scholars from many fields—anthropology, zoology, ecology, ethnology, psychology, veterinary medicine, and others.

Topics studied include how animals fit into human societies and how people in world cultures vary in their views and treatment of animals. Perhaps as this relatively new field of study progresses we may learn more about how pets came to hold a place in our families and our hearts today. Archaeologist Pat Shipman, for example, in her book *The Invaders* (2017) offers the hypothesis that Neanderthals were outcompeted in hunting by *Homo sapiens* during the Upper Paleolithic in Europe. In her view, this success was in part because these early *Homo sapiens* hunted with dogs. The hypothesis is based on data from contemporary wolf studies—using what we know of animal behavior today as an approach to understanding the past. She doesn't have paleontological evidence for her conjecture, but it is provocative.

Kisha is barking outside my front door. She and Judy have arrived, ready for our evening walk. I give Mr. Darwin—who is sleeping atop papers next to my computer—a quick caress and tell him I'll not be gone long.

Challenge: Write a hypothesis as to why dogs and cats are treated like family members.

Thinking It Through
- Identify several ways that today's pet owners treat their dog or cat like a child.
- Discuss an example of how you were enculturated to have your current attitude toward dogs or cats.
- Describe a scenario of how early *Homo sapiens* developed a symbiotic (mutually beneficial) relationship with wolves or similar canine animals.

Anthropological Terms

age-set	ethnocentric
anthrozoologist	pantribal sodality
anthrozoology	sodality
bands	state
cultural values	tribe
enculturation	

Thinking Practically

- Identify two concerns you might have relating to dogs if you travel to an island in French Polynesia where wandering dogs are common and attitudes toward them differ from those in your home town. How might you explain the differences to a traveling companion using the perspective of the culture concept.

- Discuss how the subculture of dog fanciers serves its participants much like sodalities work in tribal societies.

- Identify two reasons that enjoying cats in a cat tearoom or bar makes more sense than owning one.

17 ~ Move!

A newspaper advertisement soliciting signatures on a petition has caught the author's eye. As she reads the arguments presented for citizens to sign the petition regarding downtown development plans, she ponders cultural values, attitudes, and behaviors toward exercise as well as how culture changes.

"Longer Walking, More Inconvenient Parking, Let's Get It Done Right" reads the community group advertisement encouraging residents to sign a petition protesting a city council downtown plan that placed parking several blocks away from stores, restaurants, and entertainment venues. I applaud the process of citizens working the political process. What caught my attention with this petition plea was the emphasis that the recently approved *plan would impose too much walking!* Really?

This got me thinking about the issue of exercise in our contemporary North American culture. Exercise is physical activity that involves repetitive movement that improves cardiovascular fitness or muscle strength— activities such as walking or lifting weights. The topic has several elements to examine through the lens of anthropology—*culture, cultural values, enculturation, ideal versus real* **behavior**, and use of the *comparative method.* We live in an era when frequent articles in newspapers, magazines, and university public health newsletters encourage us to move more and sit less. Fitbits and other GPS fitness tracking devices are popular. To quantify our exercise—walking, running, cycling, swimming—we are encouraged to take 10,000 steps (approximately five miles based on an average stride length of 2.5 feet/stride) a day. The CDC and American Heart Association suggest that adults participate in moderate to intense exercise for 150 minutes per week (30 minutes a day five times per week will achieve this), or 75 minutes of intense activity or a combination of these per week. How does culture influence when, how, and if we exercise?

Some time ago another newspaper headline about exercise caught my eye—"Walking School Bus to Start." I did a double take. I learned that it was a local project between an elementary school and our county health services agency. The aim was to create regular daily exercise for young school children. In addition, the program's goals were to give kids a time to socialize, to become acquainted with other students living in their area, and to get to know parents and neighbors. Parental volunteers chaperoned and acted as the "bus" by walking a specific route to the school each day (or on specific weekdays set in the "bus" schedule), stopping at specific locations, and keeping to a schedule in order to get everyone to school on time. The "driver" volunteers walked in front of the group and "conductors" brought up the rear. Students could join the "bus" much as they would a real school bus. Walking school buses began transporting kids to school in communities in Europe, Australia, New Zealand, and the United States beginning in the early 1990s. There were also biking school buses. Walking School Bus (WSB) programs are continuing to expand today. Have you heard of one? The WSB website is maintained by the University of North Carolina (National Center for Safe Routes to School of the University of North Carolina Highway Safety Research Center n.d.). It posts guides for how to develop a WSB program including topics such as how to determine interest, officials to contact for support, route selection, and other logistics.

When in elementary school, everyone I knew walked from their home to school. It was exercise. You had to live two miles from the school to qualify for riding on a bus. For me, and those students living on my block, that meant a mile of walking every day to school and another mile home, carrying our books in our arms (no backpacks, they were "way not cool"). It was the same in high school, but in high school, the one-way walk was a mile and a half. We complained, but we enjoyed the social interaction with other students who lived nearby.

Employing the comparative method when viewing exercise across cultures is illuminating. Data from foraging and horticultural societies whose lifeways were recorded by anthropologists beginning in the nineteenth century provide perspective. Exercise characterized much of the daily life of these ancestral populations. Men among the South African Ju/'hoansi San foragers, for example, were reported by Richard Lee (2013) to walk or run several miles in the quest for food. Women carried babies, mongongo nuts, a dietary staple, and other plant foods, plus firewood and water containers (hollowed gourds or ostrich eggs), often walking miles while foraging. These were carried in a leather devise called a *kaross* that draped over the wearer's back and tied at the waist, forming a pouch. A special baby sling lined with absorbent plant materials fit inside the *kaross*; older toilet-trained children rode on an adults' shoulders. Ethnographer Napoleon Chagnon (1997) reported that Yąnomamö women of Amazonia walked miles every day in the constant quest for firewood that they had to chop and then carry back to their *shabano* (village). In horticultural societies such as in Papua New Guinea, Dugum Dani people walked to their fields carrying their tools. They prepared soils, planted, weeded, and harvested (primarily sweet potatoes) by hand. Water from hand-dug communal wells characterized the technology of many aboriginal cultures; water drawn from wells was then carried to each abode. Photographs of women carrying large water vessels on their heads are seen in travel brochures and in the media coverage of some world cultures today. Do the viewers of such photographs recognize this unending daily task as exercise? Consider walking even a quarter mile to a well in your neighborhood in order to fetch and carry back all of your drinking, food preparation, and bathing water.

Many food acquisition activities of both foragers and horticulturalists were, in addition to providing daily exercise, opportunities for social interaction. Ju/'hoansi San women often went with others to gather the abundant, highly nutritious, and tasty mongongo nuts; these were available in all months of the year. For the Dugum Dani men often worked on tasks in groups, such as building mud mounds for growing sweet potatoes and the irrigation channels that watered them. This did not lighten or shorten the physical task of hand scooping mud, but it gave a socializing component to the work. Do we perform food gathering tasks (going to the market) or yard maintenance tasks with others? Not usually. And the task of getting to school for children is more and more often a solitary ride in the family car or some form of public transportation.

Nutritional data were also cited in most ethnographies of prestate societies, including details of foods consumed. The diets of most aboriginal societies (particularly hunter/gather/foragers) provided sufficient, nutritionally diverse foods. What these aboriginal diets did not have were foods containing *refined* carbohydrates, *added* fats, and *added* sugars—all of which are common in the diets of Western societies today and contribute to excess weight gain and ill health.

Fast-forward to North America in the 1950s. Fewer daily technological conveniences existed back then compared to those available today. Families that had a lawn rarely had a power mower; they pushed a manual mower and it was exercise. There were no inexpensive leaf blowers; raking leaves was exercise. If you lived or worked in a city building of numerous stories you climbed stairs several times a day; elevators were not ubiquitous. Stand mixers that could knead bread were a rarity; kneading bread dough was exercise. Laundry was hung outside on lines to dry; lifting baskets of wet clothing and then raising your arms as you repeatedly hung items was exercise. You get the idea; ask elders you know for more examples. No one thought about recreational exercise for fitness. When we played ball or swam at the community pool it was for fun and socializing.

Now it is 2019. In our homes, technologies' "smart helper platforms" provide us with Amazon's Alexa, Google's Google Assistant, and Apple's Siri. Operated by voice recognition, these helpers perform a variety of tasks eliminating the need to exercise one's fingers—no more keyboarding, pushing buttons, or flipping switches—nor do you need to get up and walk to the light switch. Domestic robots can now help with domestic chores around the home—iRobot Roomba vacuums and iRobot Braava mopping robots clean floors, Winbot cleans windows, and Robomow mows lawns—eliminating what was part of our daily exercise.

Today's contemporary society has evolved in ways that create exercise activities that are *separate* from meeting basic human needs. People "workout," at a health club or gym, go cycling, running, walking, or elect to exercise at home in front of their televisions following a work-out DVD. Many of these forms of exercise are not social—while working on machines at the health club people watch the television screen on the wall in front of them or listen to music or podcasts on their smartphones. Zumba and other group exercise classes have a social component, but it primarily takes place briefly before and after class. I belong to a gym and participate in such separate exercise activities, in addition to the joys of a daily walk through my neighborhood. I am a devotee of water aerobics. Our instructor Ashley choreographs ever-changing routines to a background of popular music. This workout targets cardio plus whole-body isometric and isotonic muscle work in saggital, frontal, and transverse planes of movement with water creating the resistance; we rarely have enough surplus breath to chat. The separate nature of exercise activities is now part of our culture—our learned attitudes and behaviors associated with exercise.

Culture can change attitudes toward what is ***ideal behavior*** (what we should do), in this case exercise, but what people actually do (***real behavior***), may differ considerably. Exercise, according to today's doctors and scientists, can improve the quality, and perhaps the length, of life—evidence points to exercise as beneficial to one's heart, lungs, emotional and mental health, as well as being helpful to those with ailments such as diabetes. The benefits of exercise are brought to our attention daily by various media in an attempt to get us to comply with the ideal of exercising. But do people pay attention? Recent studies suggest that it is *not how much or how intense* one exercises but rather the *frequency* of movement that is important to good health. A study in the *Annals of Internal Medi-*

cine reported, for example, that long bouts of sedentary time are associated with higher mortality rates regardless other factors such as exercise habits, cardiovascular risk factor, weight, age, sex. (Diaz et al. 2017) The study concluded that getting up and moving every 30 minutes may protect against this health risk. A 2018 report in the *Journal of the American Heart Association* indicated that even short bouts of moderate to vigorous exercise (even ones lasting only 5 or 10 minutes) that added up to a total of 40 minutes of exercise per day were beneficial and reduced the death rate over time (Saint-Maurice et al. 2018). Get up, move!

The issue of exercise from an anthropological perspective is about our culture and the attitudes, values, and behaviors we learn and share. We've identified both barriers to and stimulants for change, and awareness of these may help us to alter our behaviors. Common barriers include issues such as relative values, tradition, and fatalism. Relative values would be a person saying, "I hear the message about exercise but I don't enjoy it so I don't do it," or "I don't have the time to exercise; besides I'd rather be surfing the web." Tradition may be a barrier if traditional clothing such as long robes or a turban makes exercise uncomfortable or impractical. The barrier of fatalism would have someone saying, "It is in my DNA to be heavy; what will be will be, exercise can't change that." The number one stimulant for culture change is a desire for economic gain (others include desire for prestige, nationalistic pride, and competition). Individuals may not perceive exercise as an avenue to economic gain, although this is a shortsighted view when one considers future health care costs to themselves and society. I submit that more people would exercise more if, in addition to health benefits, financial rewards were emphasized. Demonstrate that you checked in to your health club on a regular basis to receive a discount on your health insurance costs, for example. Such a program might motivate people to exercise. Institute competition between corporate departments or between school classes for most miles walked in a month. Over time, the behavior of simply walking more might become a mainstream value within our culture. If you are thinking that these are impractical ideas, reflect on why you reacted this way. Does your culture or subculture dictate how you feel about walking as a mode of transportation? How do you feel about walking several blocks from where you park your car to a movie theater, concert venue, or restaurant? I'm not signing the petition.

Challenge: Interview an elder in your culture (someone over 65 years old). Compare the number of ways you use your body in daily food getting and household maintenance activities with what the elder describes about her or his youth.

Thinking It Through

- Discuss two issues that would be raised in opposition to a WSB in your neighborhood. Describe the anthropological response you would offer.
- In the opening paragraph the city council plan is criticized by a group of citizens. Discuss how the council might respond using an anthropological perspective.
- Identify the benefits a company would achieve if their employees were given a financial incentive to exercise on a regular basis.

Anthropological Terms

enculturation	ideal behavior
comparative method	ideal versus real behavior
cultural values	real behavior
culture	

Thinking Practically

- Evaluate the benefits of people walking more.
- Discuss how social time might be incorporated into exercise activities.

18 ~ Food for Thought

Foodie experiences in an urban supermarket are explored in comparison with the food acquisition process of aboriginal foraging peoples. The elements of a cultural econiche and cultural knowledge are discussed in relation to how we obtain food every day.

A manufactured, shiny metal shopping cart in place of a handcrafted woven string bag or basket is the vessel for collection. A built-in child seat on the cart substitutes for a chest-sling child carrier. Plant and animal foods—sources of protein and carbohydrates—are found in this man-made environment. There are cement walls, tile floors, bright lights in the ceiling overhead, air conditioning vents, shelves, and display bins in this food source place. For the ancient *forager* there was sky, earth, and sunshine; wild growing plants with greens, nuts, fruits, and seeds; and animals on hoof, wing, and fin that provided the ingredients for a meal. As I enter my local supermarket this morning it is against a backdrop of our ancestors foraging for food. My anthropological lens seems always to filter what I experience. The comparative method is strong in anthropology and offers interesting perspective. Here is some food for thought.

The contemporary *foodie* forager enters the foraging environment clutching "shopping lists" and coupons, having planned family meals for a week or more, or a menu for a special meal; ancient *aboriginal* foragers entered their foraging environment with mental lists of what foods were currently available. The ancient foragers knew the surrounding topography and all of its *econiches*; they knew what grew where—plants that ripened weeks earlier in one locale than another due to soil and sunlight differences. The contemporary foodie forager knows the topography of his or her foraging place too, right down to specialized econiches—the organic produce section, the international foods section, specialty cheeses, bulk grains, gluten-free foods, chocolate. While the majority of food stores place these items in locations and by categories that I've just noted, some use alternative locations. This can cause the foodie some confusion until she or he switches her or his thoughts to other likely locations within the store.

Prehistoric foragers did not make lists, although they did often set out to gather specific foods. For example, the ancestors of the Washo of the northern Great Basin region of western North America knew in what season wild lettuces grew and where to find them; they knew the location where chokecherries ripened first. They recognized the season when fish-spawning runs began in Lake Tahoe and local streams, and the location and time to harvest pine nuts. The Washo may not have known the altitude where the piñon pines grew, as scientists do today, but they knew the location of the trees and just when to go there to harvest. The San Ju/´hoansi of Africa's Kalahari Desert knew which specific sprout told of an edible root beneath the soil and the location of trees bearing mongongo nuts and when to harvest them. Native peoples the world over who foraged for survival knew. Contemporary foodies know when nearby farms open for picking by consumers—e.g., blackberries, blueberries, strawberries, peaches, and apples.

The forager of old could identify hundreds of specific local plants and their uses; the foodie can identify and use hundreds of ingredients obtained from both local and international sources. But most contemporary cooks go to markets to obtain their foods and few know or can identify edible wild plants in their region. The true gourmand, however, may go out to collect mushrooms in the spring and can distinguish various kinds of these fungi.

The prehistoric forager as well as those existing during historic times also had intimate knowledge of how to locate and acquire meat protein in their particular habitats. Hunting and fishing techniques relied on knowledge of the habitats and the lifeways of animals—mammals such as deer, giraffes, antelopes, or rabbits; reptiles such as the large chuckwalla and other lizards gathered by the Washo and snakes of all types; fish in fresh and salt waters; birds (where they nest and when they migrate); and amphibians such as frogs. Spear, trap, blowgun, and bow and arrow were the foragers' hunting tools. These required different techniques than the high-power hunting rifles of today. The Washo, for example, would stalk mule deer while wearing a disguise—a stuffed deer head and deer body skin draped over the hunter's shoulders—that allowed them to creep close enough to herds to use their bow and arrow or spear.

The collection of insects also contributed nutritionally to the diet of foragers. Ants, locusts, termites, spiders, ants, and others are nutritious, many containing 20 to 60 percent protein, more protein than chicken, beef, or pork that are only 17 to 23 percent protein. While most North Americans today generally shun insects, other contemporary peoples in Mexico, China, and Africa regularly collect, sell, and eat them.

The ancient Washo foragers drew on knowledge, verbally transmitted generation to generation to prepare their foods. Both men and women gathered foods such as piñon nuts, but women generally did the most food preparation. They used a bedrock mortar and an elongated stone pestle to grind acorns; other seeds and nuts were ground on a flat stone. The women wove a variety of baskets including tightly woven ones used for cooking—liquids were brought to a boil by adding heated stones. Tool kits also included an obsidian knife, an acorn cooking paddle, and a fire drill to create fire. A woman or her spouse made all of these tools.

The foodie (who might be female or male, but for the sake of ease I use the feminine pronoun), too, knows how to process the foods she gathers, drawing on all of the experiences of her ancestors and those of the entire world through verbal transmission from relatives, friends, and television chefs. She also has access to written information in cookbooks and on the internet, as well as YouTube videos, to advise her. She can take a cooking class or enroll in a culinary institute. Food preparation technology today includes steel knives, food processors, professional mixers, gas and electric cook tops, ovens that broil and bake, and microwaves—all mass produced and easily accessible in the kitchen. Today's cook has access to ancient and historical tools too—woven Chinese bamboo steam baskets, European butter bells, and woks.

Techniques for food preservation were used in the past. Prehistoric foragers dried fish, meat, and fruits. They built above- and belowground caches to store and preserve nuts and other foods for winter usage. Contemporary foodies freeze, can, and dry foods for future use. Interestingly drying (dehydrating) foods at home is making a comeback as some foodies strive to make the most of seasonal, locally produced foods. Most use purchased electrical dehydrators rather than relying on the sun as prehistoric and historic foragers did and still do.

Foragers knew how to make edible food out of bitter and sometimes poisonous plants. The Washo, and other native North American peoples, developed methods to leach tannic acid out of bitter acorns, yielding a meal high in nutrients. Manioc was leached similarly by peoples in the Amazon/Orinoco River basins in South America. Today, we generally shun such foods as being too labor-intensive to produce, though descendants of foragers will sometimes continue the practice.

My cart is full; I pay the clerk and head to my car. My family will eat well tonight. The voice in my head will continue to contemplate how far humanity has come with regard to obtaining a meal. I hope that these musings have given you some anthropological food for thought.

Challenge: The next time you are in a supermarket think of a way that the store could logically be completely reorganized in the placement of food items.

Thinking It Through

- Compare knowledge-based food acquisition between contemporary shoppers and foragers.
- Contrast the strategies used by foragers and contemporary urban dwellers in the quest for food.

Anthropological Terms

aboriginal

econiche

foodie

foragers

Thinking Practically

- Compare and contrast the strategies used by contemporary supermarket foragers and aboriginal foragers to determine what is on the menu for a meal.
- Contrast foragers' and foodies' knowledge about the sources of the foods they eat.

19 ~ Who Has the Power?

Power and authority within society are complex. This essay addresses how persuasive power may lead to societal changes as illustrated with the case of valley fever.

A letter to the editor from an orthopedic surgeon appeared in our local paper this morning (October 2012). He recounted his effort to bring about changes to the San Joaquin Valley Air Pollution Control District regulations affecting local farmers. The doctor was concerned about local increases in cases of valley fever (coccidioidomycosis). Valley fever is a fungal infection that is caused by the fungi *Coccidioides immitis* or *C. posadasii* (kok-sid-e-OY-deze). The fungi live in soils and enter the body by inhalation; infection starts in the lungs. Most individuals who contract valley fever (30–60 percent) experience mild to severe flu-like symptoms—cough, fever, night sweats, rashes. After they recover they will have a specific immunity to reinfection. The initial illness may, however, develop into a chronic and disseminated coccidioidomycosis. If the infection spreads to other parts of the body, it can be quite serious and lead to lifetime debilitation or death. It can affect the lungs, skin, bones, joints, tendons, liver, heart, brain, or membranes that protect the spinal cord and brain (causing meningitis—the most potentially deadly complication). Lung involvement can cause lung nodules that are sometimes misdiagnosed as lung cancer because they look like cancer on X-rays.

The letter caught my eye because I emphasize to my college archaeology students each semester that valley fever is a potentially serious issue for those digging at archaeological sites in California's San Joaquin Valley (locally called the Central Valley) and parts of the American Southwest. Arizona and California have the highest number of cases reported annually according to the Centers for Disease Control. Archaeological field schools that operate where valley fever is present usually require that students obtain a skin or blood test that shows they have immunity (antibodies) to valley fever before they are accepted into such programs. Universities do not want to be held liable should a student become seriously ill or die from the disease. Experts estimate that 50 percent of people living in areas where valley fever is common have had the infection.

The fungus is endemic to and thrives in dry, arid soils in locations with arid summers and mild winters—California (particularly the southern region of the San Joaquin Valley), Arizona, New Mexico, Utah, Nevada, Texas, northern Mexico, and parts of Central and South America have many documented cases of valley fever. Soil disturbance where the fungi reside causes airborne spores that can travel hundreds of miles. People regularly exposed to dust—agricultural workers, construction workers, archaeologists, paleontologists, and military personnel on field exercises—are most at risk. Anyone who is outdoors, such as gardeners, runners, cyclists, or children playing, may be exposed to disturbed soils, particularly when there is wind. It is estimated that 150,000 adults and children contract this disease annually.

Nut crops represent one of the largest farm crop revenues for California's Central Valley growers. The harvesting of nuts is done by mechanically shaking each tree and sweeping the ground with specially equipped tractors to gather the fallen nuts. The process results in enormous clouds of dust (plus the soil fungal spores) and creates dirty air that hovers over the region for weeks.

In his letter, the doctor said that he took his concern about this source of valley fever to the San Joaquin Valley Air Pollution Control District. He also submitted to them a suggestion for a partial solution—

146

spread canvas aprons under trees during the shaking process. Nuts would then be loaded from the canvas into trucks. Clearly this solution would be more labor intensive and thus more costly to the farmers and ultimately to consumers, although it would greatly reduce dust-borne fungus. He was told that the Farm Bureau was too powerful in California politics for there to be any chance that the air pollution control district would lobby the state for such changes.

My anthropological lens immediately kicked in as I thought about the issues of power and authority in politics. What exactly is *politics*? Most people define it based on their own perspective or that of their culture. There is tremendous variation in what is considered political from one society to another. In traditional tribal societies what we would consider politics and leadership is most often confined to the use of *power*. In contemporary, industrial societies politics is about the means of selecting leaders to whom we give the *authority* to make decisions for our communities. Power and authority within a community determine how decisions are made.

Power involves the ability to influence or cause people to do things they would not otherwise do. Two types of power exist: *persuasive power* and *coercive power*. Persuasive power involves the use of argument, ideology, wealth, reputation, and other attributes to influence people. Coercive power involves the use of force. Authority on the other hand is the use of *legitimate* power to make decisions—power that has been vested in a person or persons by the community. We have given leaders the right to rule, and the society agrees to abide by their decisions.

The letter-writing doctor tried to use his *persuasive power* (based on his medical background and experience plus arguments about the dangers of valley fever) to influence the San Joaquin Air Pollution Control District. He, in turn, wanted them to use their *authority* to curb the current practices of the nut-harvesting farmers. The air pollution control districts are given authority by the state to implement the laws that the state legislature has enacted. At this time there was no relevant state law that the district could implement, and hence no sanctions that they could impose.

Further, they told the doctor that the Farm Bureau was too powerful (persuasive power driven by economics) to allow or support the passage of state laws on this issue.

Perhaps the doctor would have had more success in starting a dialogue about the issue of valley fever and harvesting techniques had he first gained the support of, for example, the American Medical Association and health providers who in turn would bring more persuasive power to bear with state legislatures on this issue. Or perhaps he hoped that his letter would motivate others to persuade their state representatives to act on legislation.

According to the September 13, 2012, posting on *California Healthline*, the NIH (National Institutes of Health) reports that more people are affected by valley fever than West Nile virus and it is more costly. Yet, research on valley fever is receiving only about 4 percent of the funding that West Nile research gets (www.californiahealthline.org/articles/2012/9/13/experts-say-valley-fever-cases-at-epidemic-levels-in-some-areas-of-calif.aspx). Why? Perhaps not enough persuasive power is being brought to bear on this issue.

It took decades to instigate rules about tobacco smoking even when the negative effects on thousands of people annually, both smokers and those who were exposed to secondhand smoke, were known. Who wielded successful persuasive power for years *against* the implementation of tobacco regulations? How was that issue finally turned around? Smoking bans began in the United States in 1964 when the United States Surgeon General published a report on the adverse effects of smoking. The power of his position and credentials turned national attention to the issue in terms of both health and economic costs. Within a year federal legislation was passed requiring health warning labels on cigarette packages, and a few years after that, cigarette advertising was banned on television. Over the next 40 years many additional laws were passed federally and by individual states. I recall trying, in the 1960s, to start dialogue on my college campus to ban smoking in buildings. My little group of colleagues was ineffective—we had no persuasive power. Our group did not have a medical degree or money to start a campaign to restrict smoking on our campus. It still amazes me how the persuasive power of the surgeon general started an avalanche that brought about widespread smoking bans, given the wealth of the tobacco industry and their lobbyists. Now, our campus allows no smoking inside any building and restricts how close a smoker can be to a building entrance. It wasn't quick, but it happened for the better health of us all. Perhaps the same will happen with funding to aid in curing valley fever or at least mitigating environmental dust issues.

Two weeks have passed since I saw the initial letter discussed above. This morning another letter to the editor appeared. This was from a local man who called for more awareness of valley fever. He was recovering from many of the debilitating side effects of a bout with valley fever, including misdiagnosis by five doctors and unnecessary surgery for lung cancer (misdiagnosed by X-rays). A simple blood test finally pinpointed valley fever fungi as the cause of his ailments. I wondered if more such letters from patients and doctors might stimulate enough persuasive power that valley fever will receive more research money and lead to laws aimed at reducing airborne dust.

Think how you can employ effective persuasive power to bring about change in a health-related issue in your workplace or community when you do not have any authority.

Postscript

A month after I wrote this essay the local paper ran an editorial (November 20, 2012) calling for support in finding a cure for valley fever with more research for the development of a vaccine and greater efforts to inform the public with awareness campaigns such as those for flu viruses. No mention was made of measures to reduce exposure to the fungus responsible, as was called for by the doctor's letter. Does this reflect the power of the agricultural community?

An article headline (April 30, 2013) in the local paper read, "Valley fever deaths spark call to move at-risk inmates." The article states that the state of California knows about the problem of valley fever and that two prisons in the southern part of the San Joaquin Valley place inmates at risk for contracting valley fever. It is known that black and Filipino populations are more susceptible to valley fever infection as are groups such as those with depressed immune systems (individuals undergoing chemotherapy or infected with HIV). Hundreds of inmates have been hospitalized with valley fever and complications from valley fever—thus increasing the state's cost of incarcerating its felons. Estimates are that California already spends about $23 million each year to treat members of the prison population who become infected with the fungus and require hospitalization. A June 18, 2013, news article and an editorial (June 20, 2013) column reported legal issues associated with moving at-risk prisoners. In the last seven years more than 40 inmate deaths were allegedly caused by primary or secondary conditions associated with valley fever. While the prison system has made efforts to decrease dust and educate inmates and employees, these have not been very effective. Now federal officials (people with authority) have ordered high-risk inmates to be moved out of those two prisons. This would involve the movement of thousands of inmates to other already overcrowded state penal institutions. The cost to taxpayers in an already financially overburdened state would be substantial. No mention was made in these articles of agriculture's role in the incidence of this disease. Who has the power?

Update 2019: Thousands of California prison inmates have been relocated to prisons out of the endemic regions for valley fever (coccidioidomycosis). There are reports in the news of an upswing in the number of reported cases of valley fever statewide in the last two years. There were 2,323 cases reported by the California Department of Public Health (CDPH 2018) for the first quarter of 2018 compared to 801 cases for the same period in 2017 and 650 cases in 2016 (NES 2018). There is still no vaccine for valley fever. Efforts *have* been made to increase public awareness of the *Coccidioides* fungus and how it is spread. Agricultural soil disturbance *is* listed as one source of the release of fungi spores into the air, but no mention is made of any efforts to curb the agricultural cause of dust during nut harvesting as urged by the physician in the 2012 letter to the editor. Who continues to have the power?

Challenge: The next time you read about a health issue, use an anthropological lens and analyze how power and authority relate to its prevention and treatment.

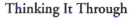

Thinking It Through
- Examine approaches to the use of power.
- Identify specific community-based issues embroiled in the use of power and authority.

Anthropological Terms
authority
coercive power
persuasive power
politics

Thinking Practically
- Using the terms "power" and "authority," compare and contrast the effectiveness that a celebrity and a local city mayor would have in changing how and where people text on their phone.
- Identify two individuals who have power and two individuals who have authority on your college campus. Discuss the roles that each would have in establishing rules affecting students on your college campus.
- Outline specific ways that ordinary citizens could help to bring about changes in the laws that govern dust production in California's Central Valley. Be sure to incorporate the issues of power and authority in your discussion.

20 ~ Potlatch?

Potlatch customs in several aboriginal cultures provide a back-drop for what the author calls contemporary social potlatch. Several features and functions of potlatch are applied to every-day occurrences in contemporary North American society.

Have you participated in a potlatch lately? Do you strive to be a Big Man or Big Woman? You and I may not be giving away pigs, shells, or blankets, or throw lavish feasts, but we all participate to some extent in what I call the contemporary social potlatch dance.

According to *The Dictionary of Anthropology*: "Potlatch is a Nootka Indian word for 'gift' that describes a competitive gift exchange in which contenders for social rank organize elaborate feasts that include large distributions of possessions, and sometimes their destruction, in order to enhance the givers' prestige" (Barnfield 1997: 372).

The term ***potlatch*** was introduced to academia and the public by anthropologist Franz Boas in his reports on the Native Americans of the Northwest Coast in the late nineteenth century, particularly the Kwakiutl. At its center were feasts and festivals with gifts. Hosts gave assembled guests foods such as salmon, herring, fish oil, and seal, as well as animal skins, blankets, and canoes. Sometimes potlatches involved the destroying of accumulated gifts in a show of what could be termed conspicuous wealth. There were many reported variations of the practice. Another well-documented and much discussed ceremonial giving custom is the *moka* of the Kawelka people who live in the mountains of Papua New Guinea. In one *moka*, 600 pigs and other valuables, including a pickup truck, were given as gifts. Such gift giving earns one much prestige and bragging rights. Each of these cultural customs involved individuals accumulating wealth objects over a period of time and then giving them away at large-gathering ceremonies. In each instance competition spanning many months (sometimes years) often spurred the organizers, and those they persuaded to help them, to arrange for more and more gifts.

Subsequent to the work of Boas and the growing data that came from other ethnographic reporting, analysts determined that, despite the variations in details, these practices served two primary functions within aboriginal cultures. First, they were a way to redistribute wealth, a leveling mechanism in societies and a way to balance available food sources—for example, heavy crop production in one region, sparse production in another. I've always thought, from my readings of early ethnographies, that this first function certainly served *people and society* collectively. This is the focus of the explanatory analysis by A. R. Radcliffe-Brown, one of anthropology's early founders of what came to be called the functionalist school. Radcliffe-Brown wrote *The Andaman Islanders* (1933[1922]) based on his fieldwork there. In this work he focused on the larger society and how customs and values served it.

The second function was that potlatch and potlatch-like customs were a means for gaining status and prestige. It wasn't a matter of who had the most wealth; rather it was who *gave away the most*. There is often intense competition among individuals who aspire to achieve status through potlatch. This second function focuses on *individuals* and what they have to gain from a custom. For example, among many New Guinea and Pacific Island societies, it was a way to become a Big Man with status and prestige. The prestige was gained through what some (e.g., the economist Thorstein Veblen in 1899) termed conspicuous consumption—in this case accumulating wealth, then showing how wealthy one was by giving it all away. This focus on how potlatch-like behavior served individuals was the analysis championed by another early anthropologist, Bronislaw Malinowski, who carried out a long-term ethnographic study among the Trobrianders and produced the classic work *Argonauts of the Western Pacific* (2013[1922]). Malinowski favored the idea that potlatch participants, especially the men who organized a potlatch, did so to gain prestige and status as they competed with men from other villages to gain a reputation. Note that status comes in two forms, **achieved status** is the focus here; it is the status you earn. The other form of status is **ascribed status**; this would be the status that you have because of the family you are born into, for example.

One of my favorite examples of the prestige/status-gaining aspect of potlatch comes from Douglas Oliver's *A Solomon Island Society* (1955) about the Siuai on the island of Bouganville, Solomon Islands, Melanesia. Oliver did not focus on or use the term "potlatch" as he described the Siuai *mumi* system, but it meets the criteria of potlatch and I've always found the *mumi* system interesting. As with most cultural customs, there is quite a bit of variation in the details between potlatch-like behavior in various cultures, yet the core ideas and functions are the same. Note that below I describe the Siuai example in the "ethnographic present," meaning at the time of Oliver's fieldwork in the 1930s.

The Siuai live in small hamlets dispersed in forested areas and spend most of their time in horticultural pursuits, mainly growing taro and with most households raising three or four pigs. The traditional way to attain prestige and status and become a leader with power, a *mumi*, among the Siuai, is to be generous. The *mumi* system revolves around the ability of a man to use persuasive power and leadership to organize his friends, relatives, and neighbors in his district to help him give feasts. Feast giving is at the core of the system. Gathering wealth for feasts is complicated and includes: collecting pigs through partnerships where you give piglets to others to raise for you, building pens in which to house the pigs, building a clubhouse for the feast where, besides feasting, pigs are given away, as many as 30 to 100. All in all this is a complex process that often takes years, and it is dependent on a man's persuasive power and diplomatic skills. There is often intense competition among men of different districts to achieve the reputation of being an admired *mumi*. When all is in readiness, a large feast is held in the newly constructed men's clubhouse. Prior to the culminating feast, smaller ones are held. In local districts people brag about their *mumi,* and there is much competition between districts over the prowess of their potential *mumi*s.

At the turn of the nineteenth century, many nonanthropologists who read of potlatch-like practices reacted ethnocentrically to the custom. Potlatching appeared to be a wasteful practice. Decades after Boas' work, further study showed the potlatch to be an adaptive practice that redistributed wealth as it conferred status on the primary participants. Ethnologically focused social anthropologists note that the custom of giving things away in order to gain status and appear as a great man or woman is a common occurrence in world cultures both in the past and in the present. The particulars usually center on economic commodities and are often more subtle than that of the Northwest Coast potlatches—at times resulting merely in enhanced status or at times functioning to redistribute wealth. This latter aspect was often reciprocal—those receiving gifts were expected to give at future ceremonies if they were able.

I submit that there are parallels between the potlatch customs noted above and becoming a "Big Man" or "Big Woman" (individuals who achieve status and power by forms of potlatch are labeled "Big Men" in cultures of the Pacific region and I use it to depict these individuals in the discussion below) in contemporary North American culture. I like to call this "social potlatch." I believe that all of us participate in this behavior occasionally. Below are examples; I invite you to contemplate them as you step back and apply your anthropological lens.

I believe that many charitable philanthropic campaigns today may be viewed, from an *etic* (outsider) view, as a type of social potlatch. I have attended many events where there are lists in the program of those who contributed money to the campaign. Names are typically grouped by how much was donated. Each giving level is often named, for example, as the diamond circle, supporters circle, friends circle, and so forth. When I read such a list I ponder why charitable contributors don't give anonymously to help the cause. When contributors are singled out, and their monetary gifts noted, their *status is elevated*—they are viewed as generous, caring individuals and their prestige grows. I don't, in most cases, believe that such giving is calculated in this manner by the giver. We are generally enculturated in North American cultures to give to help others or our communities. This value is part of our larger culture and we are known around the world for this generosity. Yet, it is also part of our culture to consider those who earn their wealth and *give generously* as being special; in feeling this way we assign them status and *we gain status* by personally knowing them and working with them. People "name-drop" about their association with these special persons. And, of course, wealth is redistributed to the community through charitable giving to aid those in need and/or projects that benefit the community.

Social potlatch using the currency of personal achievement and/or history is all around us. We give away information. We potlatch in social situations to gain status. Online gaming expertise is one source of such potlatching. When gaming participants e-mail, tweet, or post about their latest score in World of Warfare they are giving away information that increases their status within their group. When you post an accomplishment on Facebook, like finishing a marathon or a list of all of the colleges that accepted you or how many Facebook "friends" you have, this competitive information giveaway not only lets people know what you are doing, it also enhances your status. When, at a cocktail party, someone expounds on the glories of his or her recent cruise with the American Museum of Natural History, or spending two weeks building a home with Habitat for Humanity, the person's status is enhanced.

Of course it may be argued that all of this is just chitchat and that most participants don't share this information with the intention of boosting their status. This is true on one level, but I suggest that more is happening—social potlatch. The next time you encounter someone holding forth, slip on your anthropological lens and think about potlatching: giving away information to gain status.

This discussion is presenting an etic view of the functions of potlatch-type customs across cultures through the lens of anthropology.

Emic views and analysis might, however, differ. For example, I was recently at a large gathering where I knew only a few people. I was introduced to one small group of people and stood among them listening to the conversation as it moved from the topic presented by the conference speaker. Group members began to share details of their recent professional accomplishments with each other, and it was escalating competitively when someone suddenly asked what I did. Now it should be noted that I was enculturated by my parents and subculture to be modest. I generally stick to this, and I am uncomfortable tooting my own horn. But for some reason I was feeling insecure, and grew mildly concerned that perhaps the others present thought I had done nothing of note and had nothing to add to this unfolding potlatch. Suddenly, out of my mouth came a brief bio-sketch about my being a professor and that the fifth edition of my college anthropology text (with a major publisher) had just been released. I had just potlatched. Never mind that my new acquaintances had gone on for minutes regaling us with *their* backgrounds, accomplishments, volunteer works, and, in one case, a fabulous, newly purchased mountain retreat; the information presented in the conversation (competition) moved further from work-related issues as each person spoke. I smiled and forgave myself. I was doing the contemporary potlatch dance. I was giving out information—rather than pigs or other commodities—but it enhanced my status with these people who didn't know me. And I was reminded of the posture and strutting of the Big Man who had just given a *moka* in the film of the New Guinea Highlands (*Ongka's Big Moka*). Details may differ, but the outcome of social potlatches are the same—enhanced prestige and status.

Challenge: See if you can detect elements of social potlatch among people in a gathering you attend. What specifically do the individuals in the assembled group stand to gain by doing the social potlatch?

Thinking It Through

- Describe the custom and functions of potlatch across cultures.
- Examine how contemporary practices may be viewed as a form of potlatch and why.

Anthropological Terms

achieved status	etic
ascribed status	potlatch
emic	

Thinking Practically

- List three ways that social network systems (Facebook, Twitter) can illustrate the redistribution function of potlatch.
- Cite an example of when and how you've done the contemporary potlatch dance.

21 ~ Human Variation

Piqued by observations of major league sports athletes, the author explores several aspects of phenotypic and genomic variation in our species together with the implications of these to our species' evolution.

"Too short, too slow. Arms like a *T. rex* and definitely a liability in pass coverage" read the commentary under the headline, "Stand-in stands tall in win," in the sports section of the newspaper (Barrows 2014). This reference was to the San Francisco 49ers linebacker Chris Borland who had just helped his team beat the New York Giants. Borland, a player whose physical limitations were often noted both prior to the National Football League (NFL) draft and by the 49ers defensive coach, received many accolades for his contributions to this victory. He made 13 tackles and two interceptions in the game. His first interception set up a 49ers field goal. The second interception came near the goal line on a fourth-down play that ended a possible Giants score. Dream plays for a defensive player.

More everyday human biological variation, I thought, as I mulled over the implications of this case. How much athletic success is due to an athlete's DNA and how much to his or her training and practice (*nature* versus *nurture*)? Most who watch football recognize that there are big men playing in both offensive and defensive positions. Even I know this and I only watch football occasionally with my husband. But I had no idea about the extent to which professional sports teams scrutinize the players' body parts, such as their height, arm length, or hand span. Borland doesn't fit the physical profile of a defensive linebacker. Most who watch professional football would pick him out of a lineup of first-string NFL linebackers as the guy who was unlikely to be tapped to play except as a substitute. In a list of specifications looked for by professional scouts when recruiting and drafting players, a linebacker's anatomical ideals include a 32-inch arm length and a height of 6 ft. 2 in. Borland's arms are only 29¼ inches long, and he is only 5 ft. 11 in. tall. I searched for more information and found another recent compilation of statistics on 35 top college linebackers; the range in arm length was from 35 inches down to Borland at 29¼ inches. He is also at the bottom of this list in height. As I read more I wondered about the little kids who admire an athlete and want to be a professional when they grow up. How early in their lives do we tell some of them that they are simply not at the right place on the physical variation charts to achieve this goal?

I shift my thoughts to baseball and the features that might reflect human biological variation based on DNA and those that can be modified by training. Each season when I watch a professional baseball game I marvel at how batters manage to hit a slightly less than three-inch-diameter ball thrown at speeds exceeding 95 mph. I wonder if a batter's success is because his inherited vision is better than the rest of ours, because his many hundreds of hours of practice hone this skill, or because he has extraordinary reaction times. And I reflect on whether Major League Baseball (MLB) considers such issues when recruiting players as does the National Football League? Yes they do.

I decided to investigate data on variation in visual acuity. What I found is quite interesting. Visual acuity, it turns out, is more complex than I anticipated, with variables including static visual acuity (SVA), dynamic visual acuity (DVA), peripheral vision, and contrast sensitivity; all of these likely contribute to the success of MLB players. SVA is the most obvious, is best known, and is the one I'll concentrate on here. It is commonly reported with a test that scores SVA in the form of a fraction such as 20/20. A person with 20/20 SVA is considered to have "normal" vision. This means sharp, clear vision and the ability to identify certain letters at 20 feet (6 meters) from an eye chart (the distance is created in an examining room using mirrors). A person with 20/100 SVA means that a person has to be as close as 20 feet to see what a person with normal visual acuity can see at 100 feet. Typically the chart used is a form of the Snellen chart developed in the 1860s—think the big E chart with lines of letters below it that get smaller with each line. A DVA test factors in the *time* available to focus with both eyes (stereoacuity) on an object in motion.

Ophthalmologist Louis J. Rosenbaum and others began testing the static visual acuity of professional baseball players in 1992. They used custom-made tests that could determine SVA down to 20/08. This is about the limit of human visual acuity—an eagle is reported to have a SVA of 20/04. The data collected from 1,500 major and minor league players show an *average* of *uncorrected* SVA to be approximately 20/13. On the Los Angeles Dodgers roster a few years ago, half of the players had *uncorrected* SVA of 20/10 and 2 percent of them were below 20/9 (Epstein 2013; Laby et al. 1996). Such scores are statistically significant when compared to those of the general public. For example, research tests in India of 9,411 eyes found only one eye measured 20/10 (Nangia et al. 2011); a study in Beijing, China, of 4,438 eyes recorded only 22 eyes tested 20/17 or below (Xu et al. 2005). On a recent visit to my optometrist I mentioned my research to one of the technicians. She smiled and told me that her boyfriend, a minor league baseball player, had an SVA of 20/10.

Recent investigation shows that some acuity variables, specifically DVA, can be improved with specialized training and lots of practice. SVA, on the other hand, is determined by one's inherited DNA anatomy—specifically the density of cone cells (these are our photoreceptor cells) in the macula of the eye (the spot in the center of the retina). Scientists have identified a range of variation in human cone density from 100,000 cones/mm^2 to 324,000 cones/mm^2 (based on studying the retinas of cadavers) (Curcio et al. 1990). Of course you are thinking about SVA correction with contact lenses or Lasik surgery. And yes, this is true. My point is simply that we humans exhibit a range of variation that can be documented today. SVA must have been important in our evolutionary past. After all, if you are out foraging at sunset on the savannah your survival could depend on sharp, clear vision—think hungry stalking predator. Today, our cultural technology can correct faulty SVA though perhaps not down to the 20/09 or 20/10 of MLB players with this SVA.

Biological anthropology has measured and documented our species and its variation since its inception in the 1860s. This began with data such as size and shape of our 206 adult human bones—*phenotypic* "observable" features that result from an organism's genetic makeup and from environmental influences. Observable external features include those such as height, leg length, eye color, ear shape, nose shape, hair structure, and skin color; internal features include bone sizes and shapes and those features seen under a microscope such as cell form. These data are useful for comparisons in the study of fossil remains of our ancestors and in forensic work. In addition, measurement data are used outside of academia as noted for the selection of players in the NFL and in MLB and it is used in the manufacturing industry for products such as sizing for bicycle and football helmets, shoes, clothing, and car and airline seats. Further, anthropologists increasingly gather data on variation within the human *genome* (the sequencing of the DNA found within our species) to aid our understanding of ancestral populations and issues of nutrition and health today.

Humans the world over participate in people-watching and noting phenotypic variation, an activity that can evoke wonder and curiosity about human evolution. Every day, while sitting on a bus, in a bistro, on a bench in a park, or on a college campus, you and I see much of the phenotypic variation in our species, such as the range of natural hair colors, the many shades of skin color, and different nose or ear shapes. In North America most "people-watching" is done surreptitiously by glancing sideways or while generally scanning an area. This is part of our culture. It is considered rude to stare, and we are taught that it can get us into trouble if someone being stared at feels offended. Many other cultures differ in their "watching" customs, so you should be sensitive to the cultural setting when you watch.

People-watching via the media is different—bodies on a screen don't know you may be scrutinizing them. Telecasts, YouTube videos, and Facebook posts allow us to focus on human phenotypic variation, but we cannot be certain whether body parts have been altered by cosmetic surgery or camouflaged/padded clothing. I like watching the Olympic Games, for example. They afford me no end of enjoyment of the competitions and the accomplishments of the athletes. I also enjoy discussing with my husband (also an anthropologist) the possible evolutionary selective processes that contributed to the development of the *human variation* we see. World-class gymnasts, swimmers, long-distance runners, short-distance runners, weight lifters, and other athletes differ significantly in body measurements—leg length, trunk to leg ratio, height, weight, and more—fertile ground for initiating a discussion on human variation. Similarly, the popular television show *So You Think You Can Dance* gives opportunity to mull over body types of professional dancers.

Biological anthropologists have hypothesized explanations for the evolution of and variation in myriad aspects of human biology since the late nineteenth century. Did a particular feature and its size and form contribute to better health, survival, and ultimately reproductive success in ancient environments? Over hundreds of thousands of years how much did population movements and interbreeding contribute to variation? What was the impact of cultural factors such as changes in technology (e.g., tools, shelters, and medicine)? By adding a scientific twist to the contemplation of phenotypic features, one expands a people-watching habit to that of an intellectual puzzle.

All of us may benefit from human variation research in the future. Emerging medicine, termed personal or precision medicine, aims to treat patients as individuals and to tailor their treatments based on that patient's genetic characteristics (DNA). It is reported, for example, that a pharmaceutical company's clinical trials of new medicines for cancer treatment resulted in surprisingly rapid remission of tumors *for some people*; for others the drugs had no effect. In another example, the journal *Cell* reported on research underlining individual variation at the cellular level (Zeevi et al. 2015). The research project demonstrated that peoples' systems process *the same foods differently*. This has implications for personalizing diets. Eight hundred volunteers were fitted with blood glucose monitors that they wore for a week. They ate the same foods, yet their postprandial (after eating) glucose levels showed quite a bit of variation. A slice of bread, for example, was shown in some individuals to cause blood sugar to rise *on average* by 44 milligrams per deciliter (mg/dl*h) of hemoglobin; in others it rose only 15 mg/dl*h and in still others 79 mg/dl*h.

Studies also illustrate what we are learning and how it may refine our approach to personal nutrition. Research on the native Inuit people of Greenland, for example, offers tantalizing data on DNA variation and on how the body uses nutrients. The traditional Inuit diet consists of lots of fatty marine mammals (seals and whales, think blubber); yet the incidence of cardiovascular disease among the Inuit is low and Inuit seem healthy. This observation in the 1970s helped to promote the view that fish oil and omega-3 polyunsaturated fatty acids (seals and some whale species eat lots of fish high in such fatty acids) are somehow protective and counterbalance the bad effects of diets high in fat. We were advised to eat more fish, and many people began taking fish oil and omega-3 dietary supplements. More recently research by Rasmus Nielsen (cited in Zimmer 2015) revealed nearly 100 percent of Greenland native Inuit have mutations in genes involved in metabolizing fat; only 15 percent of Han Chinese and only 2 percent of Europeans have the mutations. The implication of this study is that human populations have adapted biologically (through natural selection) over time to particular diets; there were many different ecosystems and diets during the Paleolithic period (Pennisi 2015; Sanders 2015). Further research on variation such as this will refine what we know about diet and disease.

There is ongoing debate over nature versus nurture as mentioned in the opening paragraphs above. Nature references what our genes (our DNA) provide as a blueprint for our development; nurture suggests our life experiences influence how this blueprint is manifested—the role of nutrition, exercise, practice, parental nurturing, and education, for example. Is that basketball player 6 ft. 7 in. tall because of the DNA he inherited? Is it because his parents made certain that he ingested adequate protein, minerals, and carbohydrates? Or is it a combination of these? Does that woman hold the world record in the 100-yard dash because she put in thousands of hours of practice—more than other women runners—or does she have an inherited muscle variation that affects her ability to run fast?

As I ruminate on the above issues and everyday human variation, I return to thinking about baseball players, football players, and other athletes and wonder what additional variables may affect their success. What creates athletes like Chris Borland? I suddenly recall an event from last summer. At a family camp at my alma mater, University of California, Santa Barbara, my nine-year-old granddaughter was lining up to compete in the age-class swim race at the pool carnival. The announcer called for nine-and ten-year-old campers to line up. There were only two, one being my granddaughter, who was the shorter of the two. After a quick conference between counselors, the call came for the next older age group to join this heat. I looked at the lineup and my granddaughter stood only shoulder high to all of the other swimmers. "Oh dear," I thought, and my grandmotherly heart ached for her. "On your mark, get set, go!" came the shout. All of the kids dove into the pool. When they came up she was a full body length behind the leader, who was the tallest boy in the group, and she was dead last. Suddenly she began rhythmically stroking and kicking. She caught up, she passed one, then another, and another of the swimmers. At the wall she was first to touch nearly a full length ahead of her competitors. With her small body size, I doubt anyone watching at the start would have picked her to win. I smile recalling how I had cheered. Perhaps ideal size is only one factor contributing to success in sports. What about the role of elements such as an athlete's determination and "heart" (a value enculturated in North America)? Chris Borland was often described as a player who worked hard and had heart.

Challenge: Argue pro or con: Specific physical traits should be the primary factor in selecting individuals to participate on a sport team.

Thinking It Through

- What is visual acuity SVA? Cite an example of a sport other than baseball where this vision variable might make a difference in the player's success. Why do you think so? What other bodily variation might be at issue in this sport?
- Describe and compare the anatomical variation that you have noted in one aspect of the human body between athletes in two different sports.
- A recent discovery in paleoanthropology of a single fossil finger bone resulted in some researchers assigning the specimen to a new ancestral human species. In the light of your observations and understanding of the variability in contemporary humans, critique the creation and naming of a new species based on a single fossil finger bone.

Anthropological Terms

genome	nurture
human variation	phenotypic
nature	

Thinking Practically

- If personalized medical treatment developed to the point that a DNA test was required on each newborn human, discuss the implications for individuals seeking health insurance.

22 ~ Yellow-Billed Magpie

The die-off of yellow-billed magpies due to West Nile virus leads to a discussion of how observing the changes in a local bird population can help one to better understanding the idea of evolution.

"Look, a yellow-billed magpie," I remember declaring to my husband in the spring of 2012 as we traveled a road between acres of blossoming almond orchards. It was the only one we spotted that day. We traveled this road often and on many days did not see a single magpie. The yellow-billed magpie is found only within a narrowly defined area where we live in the central part of the San Joaquin Valley of California. It is a strikingly beautiful, flashy bird belonging to the Corvidae family (often called "corvids"). This group includes magpies, crows, ravens, and jays. It is 17 inches in length, about the size of a crow but with a longer tail. It has large white wing patches that are obvious in flight, and its belly is also white. In stark contrast, its other feathers are black with a dark blue-green gloss especially visible on its wings and tail when seen in the sunlight. It also has a yellow bill and sometimes a yellow cast to its skin near its eyes. I believe it is a really handsome bird. Birders travel long distances to see this unique bird and add it to their life-list of birds. We once encountered two German tourists near San Francisco. They, like we, had their binoculars and were watching birds. We chatted, and when they found that we were from the San Joaquin Valley they wanted to know what the chances were of spotting a yellow-billed magpie. This was one reason they had traveled to California. I recount this so that you know that these birds are a big deal to birders.

West Nile virus (WNV), a highly contagious virus transmitted by mosquitoes, has recently spread to our valley and has decimated this and other bird species. Ten years ago, a similar outing among the local almond groves resulted in sightings of numerous groups of yellow-billed magpies each consisting of from four to a dozen or more birds; walks in a local park that borders a river resulted in spotting many magpies and their big, bulky, stick nests in the trees.

The die-off of the yellow-billed magpies over the past few years saddens us. During 2004–2007 the California Department of Health Services WNV Dead Bird Surveillance Program reported that of the more than 800 birds they tested, approximately 80 percent were WNV positive. At that time, one researcher estimated that at this die-off rate, if it continued, species extinction could result in three to four years. Yet, on that drive a year ago we were cheered to see this one individual. If the genetic variability within this bird has resulted in its survival and if it encounters a mate with similar genetic resistance and they mate, some of their offspring may inherit their WNV-resistant genes. Should this cycle of survival and reproduction by the birds with adaptive genetic resistance to WNV continue, then the *evolution* of this species through *natural selection* would be underway. Evolution is defined as the change through time in the genetic makeup of species. And genetic variation within a species is fundamental "stuff" for evolution to tinker with.

It is now November 2013, and we drove the same road again this morning. I spied, along the way, a flock of 10 yellow-billed magpies, and another group of five, plus three lone birds. Hooray! The survivors of the initial die-off from WNV have reproduced and passed forward the genetic variability that contributed to the survival of some birds in those earlier populations that were hit by the virus. Not all species are this lucky; if there is no adaptable variation in the genetic makeup of a population under changing circumstances, extinction may result—think about the demise of the dinosaurs.

Evidence of the evolutionary processes definitively described in Charles Darwin's seminal work *On the Origin of Species by Means of Natural Selection or the Preservation of Favoured Races in the Struggle for Life* originally published in 1859 is an elegant explanation of the evolution of life on Earth. "Natural selection" is now termed a theory, which confuses some people. In science a theory is an explanatory hypothesis with *overwhelming evidence to support it*. Natural selection is supported by evidence from research on plants and animals in both natural settings and laboratory experiments. Although Darwin didn't know the sources of genetic variation or the detailed processes of inheritance, subsequent developments in genetic research provided the *detailed* mechanisms of evolutionary theory.

Darwin wrote in 1859 that (1) organisms reproduce more than their own numbers; (2) despite this tendency to reproduce, numbers remain fairly constant over time; (3) there is variation both within and between species; (4) there is competition for resources (food, water, habitat, mates) within and between species; and (5) in the competition and struggle for existence, those organisms with some advantage (i.e., favorable variations) will survive better and thus have the potential to reproduce more. Darwin based his theory on the extensive data he collected during his five-year voyage of discovery aboard the *HMS Beagle* and his subsequent research back in England. His many observations provided quantitative data to support his hypothesis and correctly pointed to the roles of variation and reproductive success as the lynchpins of evolutionary theory, particularly natural selection.

Knowledge of the processes of evolution through natural selection gives us a key to understanding and interpreting the past evolution of species. The anthropological subdiscipline of paleoanthropology (the science of studying human and nonhuman primate evolution) and the geological subdiscipline of paleontology (the science of studying other past life forms) work to collect data and unravel the evolutionary history of past life-forms. The *Law of Uniformitarianism* was established early in the history of the field of geology, and Darwin knew of it. It is the prem-

171

ise that the Earth's processes that are observable today are the same as those that shaped past landscapes. This law helped our understanding of the Earth's physical history. For example, observing, recording, and studying active volcanoes today aid us in reconstructing regions from past times that were formed by volcanic activity and lava flows. Or studying the erosive effect of flood waters today can help us reconstruct sequences of layers in ancient sediments—for example, thicker layers result from heavy water runoffs that carry soils into a lake and thinner layers of sediments result from light runoffs. All the biological sciences, too—biology, botany, anatomy, physiology, zoology, and biological anthropology—similarly use the idea of the Law of Uniformitarianism. This fundamental law, which in essence states that the present is a key to the past, is a foundation to the study of the evolution of life on Earth.

Biological anthropologists join with geneticists in research on contemporary human variation—how it is affected by our *DNA* and genetic replication processes. These studies give us data that help us explain a species' variation. This contemporary research data tell us that we should *expect* to observe variation in the hominid fossils that inhabit the dusty terrains along our evolutionary road. And we do. We can and should hypothesize that, just like the yellow-billed magpie, there were times when populations faltered due to pandemic disease and environmental/ecological shifts (i.e., weather changes, volcanism, earthquakes, influx of new predators and intraspecies competitors) that led to illness, food and habitat shortages, and death. New conditions caused potential competition, struggle for existence, and change through natural selection that favored individuals with an adaptive variation.

The recombination of genes (*genetic recombination*) that occurs with each act of reproduction provides most species variation. Additionally, faulty DNA genetic replication, that is, *mutation*, adds new material to an organism's DNA genetic makeup. There are numerous changes during a cell's replication processes that are collectively termed mutations. Most mutations have a negative impact and are selected out of the gene pool; others are neutral and may remain in the gene pool for generations before they are combined in a manner that produces a new variant in a population. This entire process is more complex than I have outlined, yet this is the essence of the process—variations are produced. Small changes that accrue over many generations lead to changes in a species' genetic makeup. It is also possible that a major mutation could account for periods of rapid evolutionary change if it is advantageous.

Today, paleoanthropologists meticulously study the anatomy of past human fossil specimens and those of prehuman primates. There are many such fossils, and though most are fragmentary, variation between fossils is apparent. We collaborate with specialists in geology and other fields to understand what environments and habitats these various fossil individuals were living in, such as predominantly open grasslands or woodland areas. This in turn suggests the types of ecological pressures involved in the action of natural selection on individuals, with new ways to move on the ground. These adaptations made it possible to avoid predators by using brains, not brawn. Fossil specimens spanning the last five million years include the following: (1) skulls of various sizes, with varying dental and facial configurations; (2) pelvises that are short and flared with features similar to our own bipedal pelvis; when combined with fossils of knee joints and femurs (upper leg bones) that are angled like ours, these demonstrate upright, long-distance walking ability; (3) feet and ankle bones, some showing slightly curved toe bones or a great toe that is slightly divergent from the other toes; one fossil with ankle bones that allowed more flexion than our ankle does today; others, including fossil foot prints, more closely resembling our foot today, with a large heel bone and all five toes in alignment; (4) hands, some with a finger-to-thumb ratio longer than ours, others with finger bones that are slightly curved; and (5) rib cages with a structure more similar to apes than to ours today (narrow at the top rather than barrel shaped). In one fairly complete fossil skeleton (the famous "Lucy") the more apelike rib cage is combined with a lower body that shows bipedal adaptations. In sum, over millions of years, we see variation over a large range of habitats and covering long reaches of time. With a background of Darwin's theory plus modern genetic evidence, we can increase our understanding of the course of human evolution through natural selection. As more fossils are found and evaluated the picture of the human evolutionary past will become clearer.

When you hear news of threats to species by some of the selective environmental changes mentioned here, or news of a new hominid (human) or other fossil discovery, think about Charles Darwin's theory. Meanwhile join me in cheering for the surviving variants in my local yellow-billed magpie population.

Challenge: When you read news of the discovery of a possible new human or other ancient fossil, ask yourself: (1) Exactly what was found, for example was it a complete bone or a fragment? (2) Is there any mention of this fossil representing variation when it is compared to other fossils from the same time period?

Thinking It Through
- Describe and explain the evolutionary concept of natural selection.
- Explain how natural selection applies to snails in your garden.

Anthropological Terms

DNA	Law of Uniformitarianism
evolution	mutation
genetic recombination	natural selection

Thinking Practically
- Identify a nondomestic animal that reproduces more than its own number in the spring. What have you observed about the percentage of these offspring that survive to breed the next spring?
- Name a virus other than West Nile that is currently killing large numbers of plants or animals.
- Explain the Law of Uniformitarianism. How might it apply to an understanding of the Earth's climate history?

23 ~ Ape Bars—Not Monkey Bars

While watching her granddaughter play on a playground's monkey bars, the author describes the major features of human and chimpanzee upper-body anatomy and their role in primate evolution.

I am at the local park with my grandchildren. My granddaughter has been working on her skills on the "monkey bars" for two months now. These bars look like a horizontal ladder with round bars (about one inch in diameter) spaced a little over a foot apart and eight feet off of the ground. Katherine stands a mere 42 inches, so her grandfather must give her a boost up at the beginning of the course.

Her hands grasp the bar from below with her fingers curled over the bar. Her thumb is not involved as she swings. Her arms are extended up over her head with her body hanging directly beneath. Katherine is doing amazingly well. She has mastered swinging her body forward and backward to gain momentum before she reaches for the next bar on her next forward swing. This particular bar system includes a 110-degree turn midway. She has learned to adjust her swing and reach to make the turn. She gets to the end of the course, does a double swing that just allows her to achieve the end platform with the tips of her athletic shoes. She starts the course again and midway her hand slips and she falls to the soft wood chips below. My mind flashes on one of Jane Goodall's famous films of her research at Gombe in Africa with the chimpanzees. A toddler chimpanzee named Flint is hanging by one hand from a flexible branch a few feet off of the forest floor. This is one of his first times away from his mother. Suddenly he slips and falls. A chimpanzee's hand is different from ours in that its fingers are much longer than a human hand proportionately to the thumb, and hand grip is therefore different. Young chimpanzees, like young children, must learn and practice how to use their body parts to swing and climb.

Observe a chimpanzee the next time you are at the zoo or view a nature video. Note that it has short lower limbs relative to its trunk. And, although its upper and lower limbs are of similar length when it walks on the ground, its arms appear longer due to its *knuckle-walking*. It moves on all fours and places the knuckles of its curled fingers on the ground, which adds the hands into the length of its arms when it is on all fours. The chimpanzee's upper limbs are muscular and, relative to its body mass, are nearly twice as heavy as a human's arms. Compare chimpanzee legs to human legs. Our legs are longer than our upper limbs, and our legs consist of more than 30 percent of our body mass, most of which is in the muscles in our thighs and hips.

The chimpanzee's anatomy is effective for a life in the trees. Its shoulder structure allows it to rotate its arms 360 degrees so it is able to hang with its arm straight above its head. With its strong upper body it can propel its body through the trees for long distances. Its long, curved finger bones serve as hooks, requiring minimal muscle strength to hold on to a branch. These adaptations make chimpanzees efficient at moving by *brachiation* in the trees—swinging arm to arm with the body hanging below. Additionally they can hang beneath a branch with one arm while reaching and feeding on fruit. Chimpanzees also have an opposable big toe and a flexible ankle joint that allow grasping with their feet, so sometimes they also use their lower bodies to help move through the trees. In forested natural habitats chimpanzees move, feed, and sleep in the trees. In habitats where trees are widely spaced they typically travel from tree to tree on the ground by knuckle-walking, a less efficient manner of movement, because it does not capitalize on the advantages of long arms and hands and upper-body muscularity.

Human anatomy, however, is effective and efficient for life on the ground. Our heavy, long legs; short, flared pelvis; long heel-bone; and feet with the big toe in alignment point to an adaptation for full-time, two-legged locomotion. This *bipedal* locomotion frees the hands for carrying. Additionally, our hands, with well-muscled opposable thumbs and relatively shorter fingers, furnish us with more hand flexibility. But our hands don't allow us to hang on to a bar or branch for long. I thought of this recently as I watched an episode of *American Ninja Warrior* on television and saw numerous competitors fall from various apparatuses as their hands grew fatigued.

Katherine's shoulder structure does demonstrate the common ancestor we humans share with chimpanzees. We, too, have full rotation of our arms (although there are some minor evolved shoulder differences between us and the chimpanzee). We, like the chimpanzee, can hang from one bar and move to another with our arms extended above us. Of course, humans don't often do this unless they are either children or gymnasts. I nearly always smile and think about shoulder anatomy when I'm in my exercise class and lift my arms straight up over my head. Really? Really, the anthropological lens makes life more interesting everywhere.

I urge you to observe closely and study this shoulder feature the next time you are at the zoo and to compare the locomotion of a chimpanzee to a monkey. Note: chimpanzees are not monkeys; they are apes. Monkeys cannot accomplish the feat of brachiation because their shoulders are adapted to movement on all four limbs (*quadripedalism*). They don't have the same shoulder rotation ability. They are much like a dog with joints that only allow front and back movement. Watch monkeys move and note that, whether on branches or the ground, their bodies are parallel to the surface. Our family calls playground bars "ape bars" rather than "monkey bars" for this reason.

The anatomical evolution, from ancestral bodies focused on the successful exploitation of arboreal life in forests to bodies adapted to consistent terrestrial living on savannahs, occurred over many generations beginning around five million years BP (before present). The fossil record

177

over this period yields intriguing fragments of foot bones, upper and lower leg bones, pelvic bones, hand bones, and skulls scattered over numerous sites in East and South Africa. The fragmentary nature of the earliest fossils often leaves paleoanthropologists with questions rather than firm answers about these ancestral groups. Current analyses suggest that a number of anatomical combinations evolved before full bipedalism and contemporary human anatomy was achieved. Future fossil finds will clarify and resolve these and other issues associated with our evolution.

Katherine's lower limb length and weight—even at her young age—plus a lack of long curved finger bones limit the time that she can play on the ape bars. When fatigue sets in, her grandfather and I are called to play hide-and-seek with her and her younger brother.

Challenge: Pay special attention to children playing. Identify ways that they move their bodies and compare their movements with those of familiar animals—cat, dog, horse, and animals you see on television or at the zoo.

Thinking It Through
- Compare human and chimpanzee shoulder and hand structure.
- Explore how paleoanthropologists interpret the fossil evidence for human evolution.

Anthropological Terms
bipedal
brachiation
knuckle-walking
quadripedalism

Thinking Practically
- Explain why the author calls complex playground bar apparatuses ape bars rather than monkey bars.
- Describe the basic differences in arms, hands, legs, and feet between a chimpanzee and a human.

24 ~ Sidewalk Fossils

Fossils in sidewalk cement, such as those that the author sees on a Berkeley, California, street, can be a lesson for applying the Law of Uniformitarianism and the Law of Superposition in an analysis of the present and the past.

Walking along Shattuck Avenue in Berkeley near the University of California campus, I glance at the sidewalk. I see leaf *fossils*—18 of them scattered as if blown by the wind. This is a city street with cement sidewalks from curb to storefront. No trees; no bare dirt. Other streets in this city have an occasional small tree struggling to live in a three-foot-square spot of soil adjacent to the street. This is a colorful section of the city with storefronts painted a rainbow of colors and display windows containing an array of merchandise, from health food supplements to hashish pipes, from boutique clothing to bouquets of flowers, from fast foods to fad furniture.

I stop to examine the fossils. They are fossils—evidence of past life forms. A geologist would no doubt scoff at my using this term since *technically* to be a fossil something must be the remains or trace of organic life that is at least 10,000 years old. The sidewalk fossils may not be 10,000 years old, but they do represent the traces of organic life that once lived in this area, so I like to call them fossils. Looking closely, I can see the thin line of each vein in a leaf. They look as delicate as a real leaf, but, of course, these imprints are sidewalk grey. Geologists, biological anthropologists, and archaeologists use fossil evidence to aid in the reconstruction of past environments. A botanical book with a plant key for trees would allow me to identify the species of tree or trees that produced these leaves—details of leaf form and vein pattern are important attributes of plants that distinguish individual species.

I reflect that I am using the theory or *Law of Uniformitarianism* as I imagine this street lined with trees. This basic principle of the earth sciences, proposed by James Hutton (1726–1797), is that the Earth's processes going on today—e.g., volcanism, erosion, earthquakes—are the same as those that took place in the past (some state this as, "The present is a key to the past"). So despite the fact that there are no imprints of trunks or branches in the cement, based on the leaf fossils and applying the Law of Uniformitarianism, I can envision trees here where none now exist.

On impulse I enter the store that fronts this section of the sidewalk and speak to the shop owner who tells me that her shop has been in this same spot for 25 years. I ask about trees on this street and tell her of the leaf imprints. She has never noticed the leaf imprints and says that as long as she can recall there have been no trees in this area.

I return to look again at the fossils. They are in a square of cement about three feet by three feet that abuts the building. The cement is a light grey color and consists of very fine-grained material. Similar squares run in front of stores to both the left and the right. But just in front of this series of squares is another series of squares that reaches to the curb. It is more white than grey and is composed of larger granules of material and is somewhat pitted. I notice that some of this white cement is splashed over the indented line between the leaf square, and a small amount is *on top* of the grey cement in the corner of the fossil leaf square. Now we are getting somewhere. The *Law of Superposition* states that unless there has been a disturbance of some type, the top layer in a layered sequence is younger (more recent) than the layer beneath it—the Law of Superposition. Originally a geologic principle, this law is also a foundational principle in paleoanthropology and archaeology. The Law of Superposition is based on the Law of Uniformitarianism because our experience shows us evidence of its veracity—lay a piece of paper on your desk, put a book on top of it, place a cup on top of the book; the paper has been there the longest. This phenomenon is also observable in nature. After a flood, a layer of mud lies on top of soils and lawns—the mud is a more recent deposit. The Earth's history is written in this manner with layer upon layer deposited over millennia.

So my fossil leaf layer is older than the white cement layer because it lies under the white cement. I walk 10 feet along the white sidewalk section to the corner. It ends there and abuts a sloping cement section that runs from a storefront to the street. This sloping area is also white in color, but there are small bits of black and grey granules in it that I do not see in the white cement squares along the curb. This sloping cement is for wheelchair access to cross the street. The grey portion of the sidewalk also ends here and abuts the sloping cement. I am able to find small amounts of the sloping white-with-black-and-grey-granules cement on top of the white cement I'm standing on. Further examination reveals that splashes of the new white cement, with its black-and-grey granules, are *also* on top of the fossil-leaf-containing grey cement in various places. Perfect. So the sequence of deposit of the cement sections is as follows: the grey is the oldest, the white came next, and the white with black and grey granules is the most recent.

Historical records in this case would allow me to verify my hypotheses regarding trees in the area and the sequence (and even dates) of deposition of the sidewalks. For example, California passed laws that require disability access to sidewalks in the 1980s, hence the sloping access to the sidewalk is probably at least that old. And, farther down the street I find imprinted on one of the grey sidewalk squares the letters WPA 1940 (Work Progress Administration, which is a work project that began during the Great Depression). This date mark gives us an absolute date for the grey sidewalk; it is old, over 70 years old.

I smile, thinking that I had solved a small archaeological puzzle. Over 70 years ago the grey sidewalk was poured. Trees were in the area, likely growing in soil between the grey WPA sidewalk and the curb, and leaves blew down on the still-wet cement. They landed at just the right time, when the cement was the perfect consistency so that they sank in just a bit and imprints were made. Some time later the trees were removed to increase the width of the sidewalk. Then in the 1980s parts of both sidewalk materials were removed and the sloping access at the street corner was created.

The tools of uniformitarianism and the Law of Superposition allow paleoanthropologists and archaeologists to make evidence-based hypotheses. They apply these tools to the analysis of fossils, *artifacts* (man-made objects), and *ecofacts* (natural materials in the environment). Noticing sidewalk fossils and unraveling the sequence of sidewalk deposition is a satisfying science exercise. Using science in this way is particularly fun to do with a child. Using terms like *fossil* and *Law of Superposition* in a matter of fact way results in the child adding to her or his vocabulary and learning something in the process. I've wondered if such informal science experiences were instrumental in my daughter's choice of geology as her college major.

Challenge: Look for sidewalk fossils on your campus or in your neighborhood and identify the plant or animal that made them.

Thinking It Through
- Examine and identify traces of past life-forms found in sidewalks.
- Discuss how anthropologists develop hypotheses about the past.

Anthropological Terms

artifacts	Law of Superposition
ecofacts	Law of Uniformitarianism
fossils	

Thinking Practically
- Identify an area of several different colored cement walkways on your campus or in your community. Hypothesize as to the sequence of deposition and explain the evidence that you used to form your hypothesis.
- Discuss how paleoanthropologists use the Law of Uniformitarianism.

25 ~ Bricks

The recycling of used garden bricks illustrates how archaeologists utilize the concepts of recycling, lateral cycling, systemic context, and archaeological context.

The 40 red-clay paving bricks are loaded in the trunk of my car. We are moving them 60 miles to another home where they will be used to pave a small path. Why go to this trouble? Why not simply buy new bricks since they are relatively inexpensive? Culture. Raised in families who experienced the Great Depression we were enculturated to be frugal; it is the right thing to do—*reuse* and *recycle*. Many in past cultures did this too. Archaeological principles fill my mind as I imagine the future of my red bricks. I'll give you a "short course" on this background that swirls in my head before sharing my red-brick musings.

Archaeologists study *artifacts* (objects made and/or altered by humans, such as tools and pottery), *features* (immovable objects made by humans, such as fire hearths, roads, and buildings), and *ecofacts* (natural environmental elements, such as plants, soils, and rocks). They systematically excavate these materials at archaeological sites and make detailed, diagrammed recordings on grids that show measurements and the relative location of recovered items. Careful analysis of recovered materials follows. This includes comparisons of the attributes of items, their distribution within sites, dates of occupation, geographical location, and more. Finally, interpretative hypotheses about a site are stated.

Understanding present-day processes can be a key to understanding the past. Archaeologists observe, gather, and record data on contemporary human behavior to infer the behaviors of past people who created the artifacts and features found in archaeological sites. The collection of such data has been called by various terms such as *applied archaeology* and *behavioral archaeology.* This type of research aids our assessment of how artifacts and features are made in the systemic context and how they end up in the archaeological context. Living people operate in what is termed the *systemic context.* This is where artifacts and features are made and used. Researchers can ask people about the form and function of items as well as why they are used in particular ways. The *archaeological context* refers to the items found in archaeological sites. Here, only artifacts, features, and ecofacts remain, and we can't observe or talk to the people who made and used them. Moreover, most past societies had limited, if any, written records to describe usages. Behavioral and applied research includes the following points that help us to develop hypotheses about the past:

1. *Experiments to duplicate ancient artifacts.* This is done using only materials available in that past time. If we are able to duplicate an object, it is likely that the same technique of manufacture was used by people of the past. With **experimental archaeology** we have re-created stone tools, pottery, and iron implements; we have reconstructed pyramids; we have made tools and butchered animal carcasses with them. The marks on bones from these butchering experiments duplicate those from ancient archaeological sites, thus giving hard data to support the early use of stone tools.

2. *Observations of the methods used by living aboriginal peoples as they create artifacts, build features, and acquire food.* This research technique is called **ethnoarchaeology** and is sometimes referred to as living archaeology. The information gathered also gives clues to social aspects of the lives of past peoples. For example, archaeologist Lewis Binford, one of the first to emphasize this type of

research and its importance, spent many months living with the Nunamiut people of Alaska, recording in detail how they acquired and used the caribou that made up 80 percent of their hunting and gathering subsistence. His work focused on the animals' bones and their distribution (which he carefully documented) (Binford 2012). This empirical research gave archaeologists insights as they analyzed data and formed interpretations about North American prehistory.

3. *Delineation of the processes by which items in the systemic context move to the archaeological context.* The most common and obvious ways that an artifact becomes part of the archaeological context are when they are discarded, buried, lost, or abandoned. Archaeologists have identified a range of information about each of these. I'm certain that you can suggest the many ways that these processes could impact the archaeological record.

This brings us back to my red-clay bricks. In the systemic context my bricks are pulled up from a patio to make room for a garden. The bricks will be used now to build a path at another house. Someone doing ethnoarchaeology in my area today could observe our laying down this new path and ask where we obtained these bricks. The use of these bricks is an example of what archaeologists term "reuse." The bricks are still in the systemic context of the culture in which they were manufactured and are still being used as pavers. Even if I give away my bricks on craigslist and the bricks are used to build a barbeque, they are still part of the current culture. Side note: You may be aware of some recent research on creativity involving bricks. People were asked to describe various ways to use a brick. Common responses were to use bricks as doorstops, paperweights, or to support bookshelves. I thought that one of the more creative suggestions was to use a brick as a coffin for a Barbie doll in children's play. This speaks to the need for care when interpreting the use of items in the archaeological record as well as the importance of carefully recording where items are found. Technically, reuse means continuing to use an object as originally intended. When an item moves across the same society and is used for the same purpose, although there is a change in the user, it is termed *lateral cycling*. Most items acquired on craigslist, from garage sales, or from relatives are typical examples of reuse and lateral cycling.

Recycling, like reuse, is common today in systemic context. The Green Movement encourages us to recycle. Technically to recycle is to use *materials* over again rather than throwing them away. The material may be used to re-create the same item (e.g., broken glass to make new glass containers) or to incorporate the material into a different product—old newspapers used to create wrapping paper or stationery; old tires become ingredients for highway resurfacing materials; used plastics and glass are crushed and used in a variety of products; old porcelain toilets are replaced with new models, and the porcelain from the old toilet is ground to powder, added to other ingredients, and used to create new road surfaces.

I recently watched local Boy Scouts (who wore safety glasses and sturdy gloves) using hammers to demolish the old toilet that I brought to their recycling event. Yes, another opportunity for me to ponder and apply anthropology. I thought of the prehistoric American Southwest where potsherds from broken, fired pottery were often crushed and used as strengthening elements (called "temper") in new clay. Temper also acts to hold clay in place, prevent shrinkage (as the clay dries), or reduce expansion (as the clay is fired). Note that crushed rock, sand, ash, ground shell, and plant fibers may also be used as temper. Did any of these pre-historic potters hold recycling days like the Boy Scouts were doing with the porcelain toilets? Did they collect potsherds that they further crushed as temper material for their pottery making?

As we turn into the driveway of our destination, I think again of the bricks in the trunk, reuse, and the complexity of the archaeological inter-pretation process. I laugh out loud. Seriously. Might future analysis of the makeup of my particular bricks tie them to the original site where they were manufactured, or bought and used? This isn't far-fetched because brick size, chemical makeup, clay composition, and temper material all provide a profile of where a brick was manufactured. Will archaeologists in the distant future ponder their movement to this new location? How accurate will their interpretation be?

Challenge: Identify an artifact in your home or yard. How might a future archaeologist misinterpret what remains of this item if it is reused or recycled?

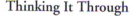

Thinking It Through

- Describe the process of maintaining artifacts in a society's systemic context.
- Examine how the everyday treatment of artifacts today can aid archaeologists in interpreting artifacts found in archaeological context.

Anthropological Terms

applied archaeology	experimental archaeology
archaeological context	features
artifact	lateral cycling
behavioral archaeology	recycle
ecofacts	reuse
ethnoarchaeology	systemic context

Thinking Practically

- How can ethnoarchaeology aid our understanding of ancient artifacts?
- Describe how a glass Pepsi bottle that you just drank from moves into the archaeological context. Is this movement direct? In what ways might the bottle remain in systemic context for an extended period of time?
- What would an archaeologist look for that would be evidence of recycling old, broken pottery?

References

Apodaca, Anacleto. 1952. "Corn and Custom: The Introduction of Hybrid Corn to Spanish American Farmers in New Mexico." In Spicer, Edward H. (ed.), *Human Problems in Technological Change* (pp. 35–39). Science Editions. New York: John Wiley & Sons.

Baragone, Steve. 2018. "Mosquito Nets Widely Misused for Fishing, Study Finds." *VOA Health and Science.* (https://www.voanews.com/a/mosquito-net-fishing/4247341.html)

Barnfield, Thomas, ed. 1997. *The Dictionary of Anthropology.* Oxford: Blackwell.

Barrows, Matt. 2014, November 17. "Stand-in Stands Tall in Win." *The Modesto Bee*, C1.

Basset, Brian. 2009, May 30. "Red and Rover." Washington, DC: *The Washington Post* Writers Group.

Berlin, Brent, and Paul Ka. 1969. *Basic Color Terms: Their Universality and Evolution.* Berkeley: University of California Press.

Binford, Lewis. 2012. *Nunamiut Ethnoarchaeology.* Clinton Corners, NY: Eliot Werner. (Originally published by Academic Press, 1978.)

Bonvillain, Nancy. 2014. *Language, Culture, And Communication*, 7th ed. Hoboken, NJ: Pearson.

Bowers, Leighla. 2014, August 13. *Combatting Malaria in Zambia, One Mosquito Net at a Time.* (https://reliefweb.int/report/zambia/combatting-malaria-zambia-one-mosquito-net-time)

Bradshaw, John. 2017. *The Animals among Us: How Pets Make Us Human.* London: Allen Lane.

Brekke, Dan., 2015, October 16. *KQED News.* (http://ww2.kqed.org/news/2015/10/16/oakland-as-exec-billy-beane-one-of-east-bays-mega-water-users)

Breslow, G. D. 2018, May 23. "Plastic Surgery for the Feet: The Rising Trend in Cinderella Procedures." *Zwivel.* (https://www.zwivel.com/blog/foot-plastic-surgery/)

CDPH. 2018, July 31. "Coccidioidomycosis in California Provisional Monthly Report: January–March 2018." (https://www.cdph.ca.gov/Programs/CID/DCDC/CDPH%20Document%20Library/CocciinCAProvisionalMonthlyReport.pdf#search=valley%20fever)

Chagnon, Napoleon. 1974. *Studying the Yąnomamö*. New York: Holt, Rinehart and Winston.

———. 1997. *Yąnomamö*, 5th ed. Fort Worth, TX: Harcourt Brace.

Chen, Angus. 2015. "Here Is How Much Plastic Enters the Ocean Each Year." *Science*. (http://www.sciencemag.org/news/2015/02/here-s-how-much-plastic-enters-ocean-each-year)

Curcio, Christine A., et al. 1990. "Human Photoreceptor Topography." *Journal of Comparative Neurology* 292: 497–523.

Darwin, Charles. 1861[1859]. *On the Origin of Species by Means of Natural Selection or the Preservation of Favoured Races in the Struggle for Life*. New York: D. Appleton.

Diaz, Keith M., et al. 2017. "Patterns of Sedentary Behavior and Mortality in U.S. Middle-Aged and Older Adults: A National Cohort Study." *Annals of Internal Medicine* 167(7): 1–11. (https://www.researchgate.net/publication/319651535_Patterns_of_Sedentary_Behavior_and_Mortality_in_US_Middle-Aged_and_Older_Adults_A_National_Cohort_Study)

Durkheim, Émile. 1915. *The Elementary Forms of the Religious Life*. London: Allen & Unwin. (Reissued by Dover Publications in 2008.)

Ehlers, Lance. 2007, November 9. *The Graduate "One Word: Plastics."* YouTube. 0:58. (https://www.youtube.com/watch?v=PSxihhBzCjk)

Epstein, David. 2013. *The Sports Gene: Inside the Science of Extraordinary Athletic Performance*. New York: Current/Penguin Group.

Eskridge, William A. 1993. "A History of Same Sex Marriage." *Virginia Law Review* 79: 1419.

Foley, William A. 2000. *Anthropological Linguistics*. Oxford: Blackwell.

Foster, George. 1962. *Traditional Cultures: And the Impact of Technological Change*. New York: Harper & Row.

Gettleman, Jeffrey. 2015, January 24. "Meant to Keep Malaria Out, Mosquito Nets Are Used to Haul Fish In." *The New York Times*. (https://www.nytimes.com/2015/01/25/world/africa/mosquito-nets-for-malaria-spawn-new-epidemic-overfishing.html)

Goodenough, Ward H. 1963. *Cooperation in Change*. New York: Russell Sage Foundation.

Hall, Edward T. 1973. *The Silent Language*. New York: Anchor Books.

Jablonski, N. G., and G. Chaplin. 2010. "Human Skin Pigmentation as an Adaptation to UV Radiation." *Proceedings of the National Academy of Sciences of the United States of America* 107: 8962–8968. (http://www.pnas.org/content/107/Supplement_2/8962.full.pdf+html?sid=dedd679d-7d5f-44fc-9f65-ebf85e76008a)

Kay, Paul. 2000. "Color." *Journal of Linguistic Anthropology* 9(1-2): 32–35.

Keesing, Roger M. 1976. *Cultural Anthropology: A Contemporary Perspective*. New York: Holt, Rinehart and Winston.

Kroeber, A. L., and C. Kluckhohn. 1952. *Culture: A Critical Review of Concepts and Definitions*. New York: Vintage Books. (Originally published as *Papers of the Peabody Museum of American Archaeology and Ethnology* 47 [1].)

Laby, D. M., et al. 1996. "The Visual Function of Professional Baseball Players." *American Journal of Ophthalmology* 122(4): 476–485. (https://www.sciencedirect.com/journal/american-journal-of-ophthalmology)

Lee, Richard B. 2013. *The Dobe Ju/'hoansi*, 4th ed. Fort Worth: Harcourt Brace.

Lenkeit, R. 2012. *Introducing Cultural Anthropology*. New York: McGraw-Hill.

Linton, Ralph. 1924. "Totemism and the A.E.F." *American Anthropologist* 24: 296–300.

Malinowski, B. 2013. *Argonauts of the Western Pacific*. Long Grove, IL: Waveland Press. (Originally published in 1922.)

Murdock, George P. 1949. *Social Structure*. New York: Macmillan.

Nangia, Vinay, et al. 2011. "Visual Acuity and Associated Factors: The Central India Eye and Medical Study." *PLoS ONE* 6(7): e22756.

National Center for Safe Routes to School of the University of North Carolina Highway Safety Research Center. n.d. (http://www.walkingschoolbus.org)

NES. 2018, April 26. "Valley Fever Cases Causing Concern in California." (https://www.nesglobal.net/valley-fever-cases-causing-concern-california/)

Oliver, Douglas. 1955. *A Solomon Island Society*. Cambridge, MA: Harvard University Press.

Pennisi, Elizabeth. 2015, September 17. "Is Fish Oil Good for You? Depends on Your DNA." *Science*. (http://www.sciencemag.org/news/2015/09/fish-oil-good-you-depends-your-dna)

Radcliffe-Brown, A. R. 1933. *The Andaman Islanders*. Cambridge, UK: Cambridge University Press. (Originally published in 1922.)

Saint-Maurice, Pedro F., et al. 2018. "Moderate-to-Vigorous Physical Activity and All-Cause Mortality: Do Bouts Matter?" *Journal of the American Heart Association* 7: e007678 (https://doi.org/10.1161/JAHA.117.007678)

Sanders, Robert. 2015, September 17. "What the Inuit Can Tell Us about Omega-3 Fats and 'Paleo' Diets." *Berkeley News*. (http://news.berkeley.edu/2015/09/17/what-the-inuit-can-tell-us-about-omega-3-fats-and-paleo-diets/)

Shipman, Pat. 2017. *The Invaders*. Cambridge: Harvard University Press.

Statista. 2017/2018. "Number of Pets in the United States in 2017/2018, by Species (in Millions)." (https://www.statista.com/statistics/198095/pets-in-the-united-states-by-type-in-2008/)

Textor, Robert B. 1967. *A Cross-Cultural Summary*. New Haven, CT: HRAF Press.

Tylor, E. B. 1958. *Primitive Culture*. New York: Harper and Row. (Originally published 1871.)

United States Geological Survey. 2016, December 2. *The USGS Water Science School*. (http://water.usgs.gov/edu/qa-home-percapita.html)

White, Leslie, and Beth Dillingham. 1973. *The Concept of Culture*. Minneapolis: Burgess.

Woody, Todd. 2014, November 4. "Meet California's Biggest Water Hogs." *Takepart*. (http://www.takepart.com/article/2014/11/04/meet-californias-biggest-water-hogs)

Xu, L., et al. 2005. "Visual Acuity in Northern China in an Urban and Rural Population: The Beijing Eye Study." *British Journal of Ophthalmology* 89: 1089–1093.

Zeevi, David, et al. 2015. "Personalized Nutrition by Prediction of Glycemic Responses." *Cell* 163(5): 1079–1094. (http://www.cell.com/abstract/S0092-8674(15)01481-6)

Zimmer, Carl. 2015, September 17. "Inuit Study Adds Twist to Omega-3 Fatty Acids' Health Story." *The New York Times*. (http://www.nytimes.com/2015/09/22/science/inuit-study-adds-twist-to-omega-3-fatty-acids-health-story.html)

Index

Aboriginal cultures
   potlatch in, 153
   totemism in, 93
Aboriginal foragers, 139–142
Acculturation process, 22
Achieved vs. ascribed status, 155
Affinal kin, 107–108
Age-sets, 122
American ethnocentrism, 11
Anansi (West African trickster), 85
Andaman Islanders, The (Radcliffe-
   Brown), 154
Anthropology, holistic approaches to,
   2
Anthrozoology, 127–128
Applied archaeology, 184
Applied research, 27
Archaeological context, 184–185
Archaeologists, 183–184
Argonauts of the Western Pacific
   (Malinowski), 155
Artifacts, 3–4, 182–184
Averill, Esther, 14
Ax Fight, The, 15

Band, 55, 122
Behavioral archaeology, 184
Belief systems, purpose of, 87

Big Man/Big Woman, 154–155
Bilateral/kindred kinship systems, 109
Binford, Lewis, 184–185
Biological anthropologists, 3, 165
Bipedal locomotion, 177
Bleachorexia, 73
Boas, Franz, 153
Body image/body modification, 63,
   70
Bound feet, cultural tradition of,
   61–63
Brachiation, 176–177

Chagnon, Napoleon, 15, 25, 133
Chaplin, George, 31
Charitable philanthropic campaigns,
   etic view of, 156
Chiefdom, 55–56
Chimpanzee anatomy, 175–177
Clans, 92–94, 96
Coercive vs. persuasive power, 147
Consanguineal kin, 107–108, 111
Conspicuous consumption, 154
Contemporary potlatch dance, 152
Coyote (central/western North Amer-
   ican trickster), 85, 88
CREEDS (functions of belief sys-
   tems), 87

Cross-cultural kinship systems,
    105–112
Crown and grill phenomenon, 71–72
Cultural relativism, 11
Cultural tradition, 65
Cultural values
    ideal vs. real, 38
Culture
    behaviors reflecting, 6–7
    defining, 1–8
    enculturation and, 45
    foreign, cultural shock from
        immersion in, 34–42
    Hall's hidden dimension of, 107
    human, Tylor's evolutionary
        sequence of, 93
    making judgment values about,
        11. *See also* Ethnocentrism
    molding the behavior of
        individuals through, 62
    process of acquiring, 22
    and walking school bus concept,
        132
Culture change
    exercise in contemporary America,
        131–132
    among Macaque monkeys, 69–70
    media's impact on, 50–51
    stimulants and barriers to, 136
Culture shock
    in a hospital setting, 39–41
    from immersion in a new
        microculture, 35–40
    from returning to one's own
        culture, 41–42
Cyclical change, 47

Darwin, Charles, 171
Diffusion, 47, 114

Dugum Dani of New Guinea, 133–134
Durkheim, Émile, 93
Dynamic visual acuity (DVA),
    162–163

Ecofacts, 182–183
Econiches, 140
Egalitarian societies, nature of, 55
Egocentrism, 11
Emic perspective
    in ethnography, 26–27
    of kinship systems, 108–109
    of potlatch, 158
    of trickster category of
        supernatural beings, 85
Enculturation, 14
Enculturation process
    body image/body modification, 63
    dealing with skin cancer, 29–30
    definition of marriage and, 99
    exercise in contemporary North
        America, 131
    kinship systems and, 108–109
    learning by observation during
        childhood, 69
Eskimo kinship system, 109–110
Ethnicity, 11
Ethnoarchaeology, 184
Ethnocentrism, 9–16, 18, 45, 102
Ethnographers, 2, 4, 127
Ethnography, 4
Ethnology, 2, 4
Ethnologists, 2, 4
Etic perspective
    of charitable philanthropic
        campaigns, 156–157
    of kinship systems, 108–109
    of potlatch, 156–157
    of totemism, 96

Evolution, 170
   through natural selection,
      171–174
   primate, 177–178
   theory of, 171
Evolutionary sequence, 93
Exercise, cultural attitudes and behav-
      iors involving, 131–137
Exogamy in clans, 94
Experimental archaeology, 184

Family of orientation/procreation,
      107
Fieldwork, anthropological, 18
Fire Cat, The (Averill), 14
Food, econiches for, 139–140
Foot binding in China, 62–63
Foragers, 55, 139–142
Formal vs. informal sanctions/social
      control, 123
Fossils, 179–182
Functionalist perspective of anthro-
      pology, 93

Geertz, Clifford, 6
Genetic recombination, 172–173
Genome, 164
Goodenough, Ward, 6–7
Grade schools, totem associations in,
      95–97
Grill and crown phenomenon, 72

Hall, Edward T., 107
High heels, cultural values/cultural
      tradition of, 61–66
Holistic approaches, 2
Human anatomy, 177–178
Human variation, 160–168
Hutton, James, 180

Ideal vs. real behavior/values, 38,
      100, 107, 121, 135
Immersion participant observation,
      29
Immersion, cultural, 21, 27
Impact study, 115
Informal vs. formal sanctions/social
      control, 132–133
In-law relationships, 105–107
Innovations/inventions, 114
Interview questions, 28
Iroquois, terminological kinship sys-
      tem of, 110
Isle of Man trickster (Manx people),
      85–86

Jablonski, Nina, 31
Ju/'hoansi of South Africa, 9–10,
      133, 140

Keiser, R. Lincoln, 39
Kinship groups, 92
Kinship systems
   cross-cultural, 105–111
   definition of, 108
   Eskimo, 109–110
   "free choice," 94
Kinship terms, reciprocal roles and
      expectations regarding, 109
Kinship-based totems, 94
Kitchen elf, 83–88
Kluckhohn, C., 5
Knauft, Bruce, 18–19
Knuckle-walking, 176
Kroeber, A. L., 5

Language
   acquiring fluency in a foreign
      culture, 36

establishing rapport through, 18–19, 36, 39
symbolic system of, 5
Lateral cycling, 186
Law of Superposition, 180–182
Law of Uniformitarianism, 171–172, 178, 180, 182
Lee, Richard, 9–10, 133
Legitimate power, 147
Leprechauns, 86–87
Lexicon, 49–50
Lineage, 92
Linguistic anthropologists, 2–3, 18
Linton, Ralph, 94–96
Locality-based totems, 94
Locomotion, chimpanzee vs. human, 177

Macaque monkeys, culture change among, 69–70
Magic, 78
Malinowski, Bronislaw, 78–79, 93, 154–155
Marriage
cross-cultural perspective of, 99–102
definitions as social constructs, 102
idea and ideal of, 99
ideal vs. real behavior concerning, 100
status and role change as focus of, 100
Mano, 116
Mascot names, 92–94
Matrilineal kinship systems, 109
Media, rapid cultural change initiated by, 69
Menehune (little people) of the Hawaiian Islands, 86

Meo of Thailand, 63
Metate, 116
Microculture, 7, 27, 35
culture shock and, 41
of a hospital, 35–42
new, cultural shock from immersion in, 41
Mohs surgery, 25–27
Moiety-based totems, 94
Monogamy, 100–101
Mother-in-law avoidance taboos, 111
Murdock, George Peter, 111
Mutation, genetic, 172–173

Native American cultures, trickster beings in, 85
Natural selection, 170–174
Nature vs. nurture, 161, 166–167
Nuclear family of orientation, 107
Nunamiut people of Alaska, 185

Oliver, Douglas, 155
On the Origin of Species (Darwin), 171

Paleoanthropology/paleontology, 171, 180
Pan-tribal sodality, 122
Participant observation, 2
establishing rapport, 18
ethnocentrism in, 18
in the foreign culture of a hospital, 36
learning/using a local language during, 18–19
of skin cancer patients undergoing Mohs surgery, 25
Patrilineal kinship systems, 109
Persuasive power, 147–149, 155

Phenotypic (variation/features), 164–165
Politics, power vs. authority in, 147
Polyandry, 101
Polygyny, 100–101
Potlatch, 153–158
Primate evolution, 171
Psychological aspects of illness and recovery, 2

Quadripedalism, 177

Radcliffe-Brown, A. R., 93, 154
Rainbow, totem of, 94–96
Rapport, establishing in participant observation, 18–19, 28 36, 39
Raven (Pacific Northwest trickster), 85
Real vs. ideal cultural values, 38
Recycling, 186
Redistribution of wealth through potlatch, 154
Relative dating, 6
Relative values as a barrier to change, 136
Return culture shock, 41–42
Reuse, 183, 185–186
Rites of intensification, 76–77
Rite of passage, 71, 77
Ritual, 71, 76–79

Same-sex marriage, 102–103
Sapir-Whorf hypothesis, 19
Sidewalk fossils, 179–182
Silent Language, The (Hall), 107
Siuai, mumi potlatch system of, 155
Social constructs, 102
Social control, formal vs. informal, 123
Social class, 54–56

Social potlatch, 153, 156–158
Social Structure (Murdock), 111
Sodalities, 122–123
Solomon Island Society, A (Oliver), 155
State, 55–56
Static visual acuity, 162–163
Status, 55, 72, 77, 155–158
Stratification, 54–56
Subcultures, 7
Supernatural beings, 84–85
Supernaturalism, 84, 86
Superposition, Law of, 180, 182
Symbols/symboling, 5
Systemic context, 184–186

Team mascots, 91–92
Terminological kinship systems, 109–110
Textor, Robert, 101
Tooth and gum color, cultural values regarding, 71
Totemism, 92–96
"Totemism and the A.E.F." (Linton), 94
Translators, utilizing in fieldwork, 19
Tribal societies, kin-based, 122
Tribe, 55, 122
Trickster beings, 83–84
Trobrianders, 78
Tylor, Edward B., 4, 6, 93

Uniformitarianism, Law of, 171–172, 180, 182

Valley fever (Coccidioides infections), 145–150
Value judgments, cultural, 11–12. See also Ethnocentrism
Veblen, Thorstein, 154

Walking school bus movement, 132
Washo of the northern Great Basin
  (western North America),
  140–142
West Nile Virus, 148, 170

White, Leslie, 5
White teeth, cultural trend of, 70

Yąnomamö, 14–15, 26, 110, 133
Yellow-billed magpie, 169–174